ARRIVAL PRESS

POEMS FOR DAD

Edited

By

TIM SHARP

First published in Great Britain in 1996 by
ARRIVAL PRESS
1 - 2 Wainman Road, Woodston,
Peterborough, PE2 7BU

SB ISBN 1 85786 498 0
HB ISBN 1 85786 404 2

Foreword

Dads can be one of the most influential people in our lives. Whilst growing up we turn to them time and time again for help and advice. They endeavour to teach us good morals and guide us every step of the way on the often difficult path to adulthood. These teachings are then passed down to our own children.

The poems that I have selected for this anthology relate to all the duties of fatherhood and show all the emotions of love and bonding.

I hope you find this collection as emotive and enjoyable as I did.

Tim Sharp
Editor

CONTENTS

THE TEACHER

It's hard as a parent, I now know
To keep a firm hand yet somehow show
Exemplary calm.
And practising hard, as I have done
That tireless patience you have shown
Eludes me.

You've never had to preach
To prove that you are wise
But should I ask
Your guidance would be given
So it is, still.

And a grandpa too
I watched you soothe my crying babies
With that same quiet competence
Always there in so many ways
Throughout the passing years
A cryptic crossword, glass of scotch

What is that word Dad?
                              - Cheers!

Barbara Beveridge

MY MESSAGE TO DAD
(Borne on heavenly wings)

Did I ever tell you dad how much you meant to me?
Did I say 'I love you' as I stood close by your knee?
If I didn't show my feelings as I grew into my teens.
If I took your love for granted, or said things I didn't mean.
Then please may I apologise, and pray that you will know,
That through the years of growing up, I really loved you so.
You helped me in so many ways, advice you gave me gladly.
And through your later years of life, as your health failed - sadly;
You sometimes didn't know me as I'd take your hand in mine,
Then you'd say 'God bless you dear' - memory fleeting for a time.
Dad, my heart was bursting for the years we'd been so close.
And when you slipped away, I grieved - you'd joined your heavenly host.
Now years on my heart still yearns for those happy times now past.
And dad, those dearest memories are in my heart to last.

Anne Baker

DAD'S LOVE

When my Dad sat me on his knee,
He bounced me up and down with glee,
When we had done he put me down,
and looked at me with such a frown,
Go and play now for a while
and put me on a nice big smile,
When I arrived back in for tea
My Mum said God had taken he,
I kept on smiling just for Dad
he didn't want me to be sad
I said to God look after him
I'll keep on smiling just for Dad.

Jenny Rowles

DAD

I sat and thought about all I missed,
when I moved away from home,
how Dad would laugh and smile at me,
when I was sad and felt alone.

Dad used to sit and watch TV,
in his large floral patterned chair,
his eyes reflecting the picture screen,
his grey hair sparkling in the light.

Dad didn't dress like other Dads,
he would wear shorts or jeans,
and brightly coloured T-shirts,
with a pair of athlete trainers.

The best thing about Dad is . . . ,
he loves everyone, and they love him.

Natalie Hooper

POEMS FOR DAD

I have a dad who is from Guyana South America.
When I was little he would be at work posting letters,
I only saw him on Sundays when we would go to church.
He would cheer me up when I was hurt.
We would kneel at my bed with my brother and my mum, my dad
started with the first prayer I would say the last prayer at the end.
We also went to fairs mostly on slow rides because I was
tiny he would stand there taking pictures of me, he was
really pleased when I was born because I was the long
awaited girl that he had always wanted, he had three boys
before me you see. I love my dad and I know he loves me.

Reann Graefe

3

BRIAN

I knew my father, so it seems,
not through his hopes, nor through his dreams,
but through his work, his life-long master,
through hawk and trowel, cement and plaster.

He opened up a world to me,
a father's place most kids don't see,
so whilst at home I knew my dad
at work each day a friend I had.

He seemed a god, a special man,
a skilled and gifted artisan
whose son he filled with so much wonder,
a man whose peers all fell asunder.

In time my unskilled hands he made
an image of his family trade,
though came a time when being taught
did not sit with me and times were fraught.

A need to grow, a need to be me
urged a yearning to be free
and this natural force came to fruition
when illness axed our working union.

Now I work alone, my teacher gone
yet still my boyhood thoughts are strong;
the sights, the sounds, the smells, the same
and through these senses he remains.

Although I miss the treasured days we knew
an unexpected light shines through,
for the friend at work I long had known
is now my dad, a friend at home.

Martin Canning

PS I LOVE YOU

The fire crackles in the grate,
Flames casting shadows on the wall,
My mind rolls back to days gone by,
I smile as I remember them all.

The things we said the things we'd done,
Sometimes seem so far away,
Then I remember other things,
That only seem like yesterday.

How we laughed how we cried,
Over things we had said or done,
At times I must have disappointed you,
But you made me feel like number one.

You found it hard to show your love,
Your feelings were somehow suppressed,
But you must have had your reasons,
And I suppose you thought it best.

I could still feel your love for me,
And I loved you dearly too,
I just didn't get the chance to say,
Thanks for everything Dad, I love you.

Lindsey Jenkins

TO MY FATHER
(for his words of wisdom)

Because of you -
I am here for as long as God allows

Because of you -
The getting of wisdom is paramount

Because of you -
Everything is found in good books

Because of you -
Every special thing comes in small parcels

Because of you -
I try to be true to myself

Because of you -
I try to be good -
            and let who will be clever.

Thank you for being you.

Lily Langton

NUMBER ONE DAD

My dad is the greatest, the very best
And I just wanted to say
I love him more than anything
He's there for me every day.

He's my friend, not just my dad
When there is rain, he brings out the sun
I love my dad with all my heart
He is my number one.

He's watched me grow and helped me through
Whenever I need him, he's there
'I love you dad and I want you to know
Just how much I care.'

I love my dad for everything he does
He helps me when I'm sad
I want everyone to know that
He is a number one dad.

Maria Dudley (15)

MY DAD

I wish I had your shoulder to cry on
to run to when feeling sad
I wish I had you to rely on
when I know I've done something bad

I wish I had you to share laughter
to also share in my pain
I wish I had you to walk with
along a sunlit country lane

But you died when I was only nine
Oh why did you have to go
I thought that you would always be mine
how little did I know

I think of you often,
with memories so true
Oh my dear Daddy
I will always love you

Jenny Brownjohn

LOVING MEMORIES

I had the most wonderful Father
Who wore a white hat on his head
He was up every morning, before the sun
To bake lovely cakes and bread.

He made doughnuts with jam in the middle
How it got there he never would say
He dipped them in crystal white sugar
To serve, nice and hot, from a tray.

He made cakes for special occasions
Like weddings, and birthdays too
He would ice names on top for children
Pink for girls and for little boys, blue.

Just as the town was about to wake up
He would open the Baker's shop door
For the customers loved his tasty goods
And each day they came back for more.

In a freshly laundered white apron
He would greet everyone with a smile
If he knew anyone who was lonely
He would stand and chat for a while.

Although he was always so busy
Every day he found time for me
Then his grandsons became the light of his life
His love was plain to see.

Dear Dad, I wish you were here still
To love and to care for me
But you're never far from my thoughts each day
You live on in my memory.

Brenda Allen

I LOVED YOU DAD

I loved you Dad, all your life,
You were always there through strain and strife.
You picked me up and brushed me down,
When I ran ahead and fell on the ground.
As I grew, you were always there,
Sharing my troubles and showing you cared.
As time went on you gave me away,
To start a new life, with Barry to stay.
As you grew older, I came round to care,
To share your loneliness and despair.
We had our chats and cups of tea,
Treasured moments that will always be,
Buried deep inside my heart,
Oh how I wish we were not apart.
Parted by death, no more to see,
You standing in your garden waiting for me.

Jill Munday

FOR CHARLES

The nicest, kindest, most handsome man
The strongest truest and heroic
The man who held his little girl
And called her 'His beautiful princess'
Who loved her and protected her
And told her how good and clever she was
A man of great wisdom and integrity
A man who never got drunk
And lost his temper and control
A man whom his daughter could trust
A man she could call her champion
The man, I wish you could have been.

Julia Wallis-Bradford

9

I WISH I KNEW MY DAD

Yes, I do miss my dad I never knew
He died when I was two, so I never knew

Looking back to my childhood
I remember things as a child would

He was not there for me to call dad
at the time it was all very sad

I could not understand why he was not there
others had their dad, it all seemed so unfair

Although physically he was not there
I knew in spirit he was always there

I imagined what it would be to hold his hand
building sandcastles and playing in the sand

I mimicked my friend at play with his dad
and enjoyed the pleasure of my non-existent dad

So in a way I was a happy lad
but it would have been fun to have had my dad

He would have been kind and gentle to me
always guarding and protecting me

Ready to scold me when I did wrong
and then hold me in his arms so strong

Walked hand in hand to the playground
and watched me run round and round

Taught me how to play cricket
and even take a wicket

Told me about his first hilarious date
and joked about his falling out with his date

Bought me my first pint in the pub
and warned me not to hang around in the pub

I have done all these things with my imaginary dad
so I love my dad very much and am not sad.

Albert Moses

MY DAD IS ARNOLD SCHWARZENEGGER . . .

That's a lie, he'd slap my legs, he gained my respect for that,
but he also gained my embarrassment for wearing that silly hat (in public)
But that's what Dads are for, to crack a joke,
to 'lose' his pipe because we don't like the smoke.
To tell silly stories that make us laugh,
and to shout at us with his tongue of wrath.
To still give me money though I'm twenty three,
to say 'when you were little you sat on my knee'
(apparently my legs also used to dangle!)
I wouldn't do that now, we're not that way inclined,
but Dad's not bothered, he doesn't mind.
He's there to question boyfriends,
to pat me on the head when I'm sad.
to loathe my taste in music,
when his is really bad (classical).
He likes birds, I like cats, I've wanted a tabby for years,
He says I can have one when I'm married, 'thanks Dad, really, cheers.'
He thinks he's computer friendly, they're nearly the best of friends,
but he seems to swear at the screen a lot, that relationship's nearing the end.
My dad does try, he's a top bloke, though you haven't heard it from me,
so to let him know he's not forgotten, I've written it for him to see.

Hannah Mew

HERE WE COME AGAIN DAD

Lend us a fiver Dad
Lend us a score,
Lend us a tenner Dad,
Lend us some more.
Here we come again Dad,
With begging bowl,
With cap in hand,
On your ear-hole.
We'll pay you back next week Dad.
Next month we'll pay our debt.
Can you wait a little longer Dad? .
Only we aint quite got it yet!
But we will pay you back one day Dad,
With all the interest due.
A hundred percent of love in full,
For Father we love you.

George Warren

MY DAD

My dad is very special and he always will be
I love him very much and I know he loves me
He doesn't drink much but he likes a smoke
He's the best dad there is
Just a brilliant bloke
On the horses he fancies, he places a bet
He's won a few times but nothing big yet
The Canary Islands, it's his dream one day to go
I wish I could send him there but how? I don't know
But if I ever win lots of money then I can guarantee
The Canary Islands is where dad will be
Until then he'll sit in his chair and watch TV
My dad will always be just perfect to me.

Heather Dunn-Fox from Leek

MY DAD

What is a Father? I'll try to define,
A hero, a friend, a great love of mine.
When Laurence was born he was fighting a war,
But when I arrived, he was outside the door.
One year later came Martin, his family complete,
He'd need regular work now to make sure we eat.
If I needed comfort, for his lap I would make,
and he'd give me the cherries from his favourite cake.
One day home from school I started to hike,
When he gave me a lift on the bar of his bike.
He would lend me three shillings, some stockings to buy,
And then take it back with a wink of his eye.
As I grew to a woman encompassed with care,
If I needed a shoulder, I knew he was there.
On the day of my wedding, he looked oh so sad,
His own little girl was leaving her Dad.
It's so hard to take, me becoming a wife,
Having another man in my life.
After a while, when my family began,
My boys adored Grampa, their own special man.
Once more he was needed for his unique charm,
To guide them, and love them, and keep them from harm.
I'll never forget the day my Dad died,
My hero was taken away from my side.
Lying there quiet, a cut on his chin,
He'd open his eyes, he'd give a wry grin.
But alas he didn't, the truth I can't bare,
He'd walk in the room, he'd be in his chair.
No! He's tending God's flowers in heaven above,
So each night I send prayers spilling over with love.

Carol Simpson

MY DAD

My dad was a man,
Tall and straight.
He'd walk down the road
With a sailor's gait.

He was a warm man,
With a heart full of love.
Straight to the point
For truth he strove.

He could be strong,
Thought gentle and kind.
He had his bad moments,
But none come to mind.

Very well respected
By both young and old.
When it came to the truth,
He was always bold.

How I miss my dad,
His love and his smile,
I look at his photo,
And ponder a while.

I look to the time,
When I'll see him again,
Tell him how I missed him,
And my sadness will wain.

Josie Minton

14

POOR DADDY

Daddy, do you remember
The first time you took me to church?
On a proud, sunny day in September,
When I made your heart jump and lurch.

We sat at the draughty back
Alongside the half-open door,
On a form like a wooden rack,
That made my poor bottom sore.

Craning my neck to see
What was happening up ahead,
My hat popped off on a spree,
'Leave it!' Was all you said.

Mummy had given me sixpence,
But you made me give it away,
I just did not see the sense
Of putting it on that brass tray.

'Don't sing so loudly,' you begged,
Do not look around during prayers -
Stop staring and swinging your legs -
Mind your business as others mind theirs.

You were really cross with me,
But I could hold it back no more,
'Daddy, please, I need a wee.
And my hat is still on the floor.'

You rushed me out of the door,
No time to retrieve my hat,
You told mummy, 'I'll take her no more.'
Now, daddy, why did you say that?

Laura Carlisle

A POEM FOR MY FATHER

My Dad means more to me than anything
Than a thousand words can convey
His love, guidance and his advice is constant
The knowledge and experiences through his own life
Has made him the ever loving, but sharp and forward
                              thinking person he is today.

Sadly, his own father died six weeks before he was born
So my Dad has never had a Dad's influence or chance
To tell us happy stories or fond memories of my Grandfather
And yet, he never shows any bitterness about his situation.
Not once have I ever heard him complain or moan.

With us, at times, he can seem over protective
Obviously, we know the reason why
My brothers and I wouldn't change him for anything
We've grown up in a solid caring environment with Dad
Always right behind us and forever encouraging by our side.

Whatever he is thinking he'll tell you
Whoever you are please or offend
You get his opinion straight and to the point
Yet still helpful to all, and always our best friend.

I could describe his character forever
But not cover really all I want to say and explain
Basically we appreciate the 100% energy and time
He has always given us as a Dad and now a Granddad
it's our turn to look after him now he's retired
To keep him in the best of health, free of stress
                              or any kind of pain.

Janice Johnson

TO DAD

For your part in our happiness
For your part in our birth
Who gave us part of what we are
Who gave us life on earth
In many years of living
Of people passing by
Some gave you love and laughter
Some made you want to cry
The smiles hello
The hugs goodbye
The passing of the years
The visions of the future
Your ambitions and your fears
Two little girls then joined the throng
Of people passing through
And stayed, and stayed forever
To always be with you
In lots more years of living
Of experience in life
Through all the joy and laughter
Through all the pain and strife
Two people of the thousands
Who can say that they know you
Will be forever caring
Because Dad
      We love you.

Julia Akroyd & Elaine Jessop

A MEMORY OF MY DAD

My dad is just a memory
He was killed ere I was born
The war claimed another victim
Another fighting man to mourn.
Although I never knew him
My dad to me is real
His photo's on the mantelpiece
So his presence I do feel.
Before he went away to fight
He chose his baby's name
Conceived at Christmas, while on leave
The name of 'Carol' came.
I'll never know a father's love
Denied to me by fate;
So many of us never will
And yet, there is no hate.
It was their duty, these men of war
to fight for King and land
But oh, I do so often wish . . .
I could have held his hand
My children missed their Granddad
A gent to spoil and tease
A laughing elder figure
Some happiness to seize,
So, dad, if you are up there
And looking down on me
I hope I've made you proud
And you like what you can see.

Carol O'Connor

DADDY'S HOME

I'd like to skate across the sun
and dive into the moon
I'd like to live in a currant bun
and eat it with a spoon
I'd like to swim in seas of cream
with strawberries for fish
My world would be a living dream
If I only had one wish
I'd like to climb the root of a tree
and walk right underground
I'd like the world to wink at me
and never make a sound
I'd like to go on a rainbow ride
donkeys are a bore
I wouldn't ever have to hide
or do my Daddy's chores
I'd like to sleep upon a cloud
with Jesus very near
I'd like to scream and scream so loud
but no one else would hear
I'd like to fly high in the sky
and talk to all the stars
I'd like to never have to cry
and visit men in Mars
I'd really like to go to sleep
and be left all alone
In the dark my soul to weep
Oh no! My Daddy's home.

R Finch

DAD'S STORM DUTY

The delinquency of lightning is
It shakes wider than it strikes
The tilted beds off centre and the like.
Lucky the toppling towers -
Some certainty
Is never desolation and tonight
The fathers go round windows shutting in
An atmosphere of tense electric white.
Mild detonations linger,
Resettling the clouds to shifting sleep
For beckon-breasted women
Who forget
Necessity of passion as the gusts
Lifting the leaves along the shiny street
And rain remembered freshening
Their lust.

Alasdair Aston

LIONHEART

As rugged as the rocks you often climb
To fill your great desire for adventure,
You never flag or tire with passing time.
In your abilities you're always sure.
You are always looking for something more,
Of no challenge are you ever afraid.
You scale mountains and barren Dartmoor's Tors
As laziness you constantly upbraid.
From my childhood I have looked up to you,
You have the strength to follow your instincts.
Hopefully in me your drive will live on
So that it will never become extinct.
Richard, my dad, you have a lion's heart
And of your life I'm proud to be a part.

Chris Scriven

ODE TO DAD

The mighty animals heave and strain, the plough boy tries to forget the pain,
Of blisters on his callused hands as he calls out his commands.
'Whoa boy - steady as you go,' furrow after tedious furrow.
Many thoughts pass thro' his mind as he plods along behind
Wonders what the future might bring, soon he'll be fighting for
                                                    country and King.
Could have been you Dad all those years ago, ploughing yet
                                                    another furrow
Composing poetry as you do now, only the furrows are in your brow!
Did you wonder whether you'd have sons? Well you did, and here is one.
Writing hopefully in verse, 'A chip off the old block', I could
                                                    have done worse.
Cos when I look in the mirror, hoping it won't crack -
It's not just me I see looking back -
Receding hairline, greying hair, I think that's part of you in there.
So, thanks Dad for leaving behind that plough -
Cos if you hadn't met a certain Cornish maid, I wouldn't be here now.

T G Cottingham

LEAVING

My eyes now closed I no longer feel the pain.
Visions of flowering meadows, clear drops of glistening rain.
I can now watch the blossom blowing from the trees,
Knowing that what carries them a warm and gentle breeze.
I wonder in the garden the clouds beneath my feet,
The open arms of an angel wrap me in a sheet.
I feel so peaceful now I'm here and this is where I will stay,
As I look over my shoulder the beginning of another day
My family each and everyone of you I leave on this lonely day,
In your mind and in your hearts this is where I will always stay.
I know it's very hard but please I beg don't cry.
I have crossed from one to the next that place up in the sky.

Peter Simpson

GIANT GEORGE

High stepping over wet summer grasses,
green glistening arcs, ripe and heavy.
A toddler's eye line greeting,
a teaching, towering giant.

Dusk softening the wood shore edge;
swept up to meet the crescent moon.
A new moon for a babe,
in a loving father's arms.

A Catholic dad, greater to me than Him,
as the scent of the wood and its King,
brought me to a pagan love
of a whispering Mother Earth.

Father of mine. In protection and strength
have I grown, a tributary to your soul.
This daughter loves you now,
as a blessing; as a mystery.

Lynne Harling

THE WISH

If I could have a wish, and make that wish come true
I'd wish that everyone in this world had a dad as nice as you
There'd be no more wars between nations
There'd be peace on every street
No reason for the policeman - pounding on his beat
Everyone would be happy, everyone would be glad
But not as happy as me - cos you are my dad.

Now you've gone to a better place, where peace rules all the land
No sound of rifle bullets, nations walk hand in hand
I don't think it was your time to go, you'd so much more to give
No reason for you to die, more reason for to live.

22

He must have needed someone, an accordion to play
When He chose my dad to join Him on that St Patrick's Day
he really chose a good one, to keep the spirits high
As angels fly above us, my dad he too will fly.

To those of you who loved him, think not this day of sad
But give thanks to God for giving you the honour
Of knowing someone like my dad!

Derek Reed

MY DAD

When I think of my dad - I think of steel
He was strong, reliable and had zeal
For life - his work, he was honest and true
He had a soft-centre, seen by a few
Generous and kind, without a doubt.
He never revealed those he helped out
Many owe him their gratitude
To help others he had an aptitude
His job was every young boy's dream,
An engine driver in the days of steam.
Trains in those days arrived when due
And left the station as the whistle blew
During the days - and nights - of the war
They carried munitions, passengers and more
In the thick of the bombs and doodle-bugs
Brought the boys home on leave to us
I am so proud of my dad - he was the best.
I wish I could tell him - he was above all the rest.

Mary Lawrence

MY DAD

Memories are vivid in my mind
Of a loving father, always kind.
Then angels took you away from me
But from your pains they set you free.
You gave your help to those in need
Aiding them to a better life to lead.
For a few years only I had your love too.
Enough to last all my life through.
You taught me manners, are more worthy than wealth
Talents, less important than good health.
To laugh is better than to cry
With these thoughts you'll get by,
Now whenever things go wrong
I think of you dad once so strong.
A love like yours was very rare
I know now you are in God's care.

June Fox

MY DEAR DAD!

Suddenly, you passed away.
        You left me lone and lost!
No more will you be at my side,
Guiding me through life's highway.
        We didn't even say Goodbye . . .
        A tear doth often dim my eye,
        When I remember days long gone,
        And when I sing your favourite song!
The sadness still is there within:
        Time has healed, but cannot hide
        The love for you I feel inside.
        You were my one and only Dad
        The greatest pal I ever had!

Freda Ringrose

24

PRECIOUS MEMORIES

As you lay in the room next door to me,
Swamped in exhausted sleep,
I wonder what precious memories of you,
After your death I shall keep.

As your worn face stares at me from a shelf,
it seems that I inflicted each line.
Although your mouth still smiles, each hour of work shows,
Hanging beneath your eyes like a vine.

You are my model, my idol, my life,
Without you I would not be here.
It's true what they say, no other man in any way,
Could I compare to you and come near.

You and of course mum, taught me to laugh and to cry,
You taught me right from wrong.
When we were apart, an empty space replaced my heart,
and we won't be together for long.

When I leave home, far away from your care,
To face the world that you screened.
No longer your baby, but quite a young lady,
I'll make you proud of what you achieved.

However independent I become, however well that I do,
I'll always need you, my dad.
Your mischievous smile, your bad jokes, your funny face and playful pokes.
I'll remember all of the good times we had!

Sarah Marley (14)

FATHER TO MY THOUGHT

My inmost thoughts forever stray -
To my childhood - yesterday!
To my father - whom I lost -
In tender years - to my cost!

For eight years old is much too soon -
To lose a dad - who's such a boon!
What might have been - I'll never know -
But 63's too soon to go!

He'd seen the world - by courtesy -
Of service in the King's Navy!
The first world war had been so grim -
'The Dardanelles' - where life was slim!

So many tales he could relate -
Of naval days - his life to date!
A gruesome time to be at sea -
To help a younger world be free!

But worldly innocence is gone - no time today -
To have those thoughts of yesterday!
Yet memories will forever bide -
Where those special needs can't hide!

And I know he's always there -
I feel his strength - and know he'd care!
I'm proud and grateful that I had -
A strong and patriotic dad!

Doreen Wheeldon

FOND MEMORIES OF MY FATHER

My daddy was a soldier boy
A soldier boy was he
He fought for King and country
Far across the sea
He was a very brave young man
Won medals bright and new
But that was long ago
Now my memories are few
Our soldier boy had no regrets
He'd had a happy life
With all his family round him
And a loyal devoted wife
But soldier boys grow old alas
And sadly came that day
Old soldier boys they never die
They only fade away.

Vera Hobbs

REALLY DAD!

I know that I'm not always very good,
But I promise you I would be - if I could.
But really dad it's not that easy,
For me to put up with your teasing,
And when at home I mess around,
Or leave things lying on the ground,
Or do not do what I am told,
Or act like I'm just two years old,
You may think that you have reason to be cross,
But honest dad you haven't though because,
All the time, every day,
Wherever I am, people say
'Goodness Karen, you're just like your dad!'

Karen Maton (12)

27

HAPPY FATHER'S DAY

dreams are funny things
some people say
and I know it's been ten long years
since you passed away
yet last night we met again
if only in my mind
but this time I was walking ahead
and you were lagging behind
we walked down to the pub
like many times before
talking about the ways of the world
from door to door
I remember, you would have a Guinness
and me, a light and bitter
sometimes we would have a chaser
on and on we would twitter
in my dream I ordered something different
a bottle of red wine
it just seemed the natural thing to do
everything was fine
you ordered a £50 bottle of Champagne
and I complained
but you couldn't see without your glasses
you simply explained
too soon you were gone and I awoke
weeping as I lay
Dad, until we have that drink together
happy father's day.

Michael D Kearney

FATHER'S DAY

Highly a father
Regards his own son,
Special in all ways
Above everyone.

Watching his progress
From birth into life -
Schooldays and onwards
In peace and in strife

When school is over
Ready, steady, go!
It's bang into life
Whatever you know.

A father still cares
In his special way
When he has no power
A son's mind to sway

How much more will God
Our Father above
Study our progress -
Support us with love

When we have success
The Lord will rejoice,
When we are cast down
How we need His voice!

G Thompson

SUPER FATHER - SUPERB MECHANIC

An orange ball of brilliant sunshine - not a cloud in sight -
We packed the picnic basket, exclaiming with delight
At chocolate snowballs, orange crèmes, fizzy soda-pop,
You revved the car, we loaded up - beach ball on the top.

Through leafy country lanes - motorways were not your style -
We chatted, played magnetic games, counting every mile;
The sun rose higher, in the sky, we were hot and damp,
Mum opened all the windows, we stopped - once - to decamp.

An ominous smell of burning pervaded the sticky, humid air,
You, calmly pulled over to a patchy grass verge, where
It was announced - with a grin - a minor problem with the belt,
A search in the boot produced a hoot - and, a look of guilt.

No spare fan-belt could be found - Mum gave up her new tights -
Soon, we were on our way again, an end to sibling fights;
Sensing salt-laden air, we competed to spy the first gull,
But, it was not to be, fate would complete her cull.

Such a racket, from the bracket that held the eroded exhaust pipe,
So placidly, you stopped the car - that was true to type -
We watched, with bated breath, as you stepped round, to the rear,
From the corner of Mum's eye, fell a frustrated tear.

Your famous grin in place, between a finger and an oily thumb
You held the ultimate solution - a pack of chewing gum,
Four sets of chomping jaws - a sickly, peppermint smell,
At last, the mass - as decreed - served the purpose well.

What a day it was, eventually, we arrived at the coast,
And, for over thirty years, Dad, I have never failed to toast
Your determination, consideration - my father, a titanic,
But, dearest of all, ten feet tall, truly, a superb mechanic.

Christine Baxter

MEMORIES OF AN IRISH AIRMAN

My father never read me bedtime stories,
Recited lines from Shakespeare's plays instead.
The Merchant of Venice always was his favourite,
He acted Shylock as I lay in bed.
And often he would sing the songs of airmen,
the ones that used to cheer them in wartime.
I learned, 'Pack up your troubles in your old kit bag',
Before I ever heard a nursery rhyme.
Often he would tell of friends that he had known,
An anecdote accompanied each name.
All his amusing stories of things that they had done
Made me imagine war was just a game.
Rarely he would mention the coffins that went home,
Sealed up and to be opened by no one.
Sometimes he would speak of the treatment of the Jews,
And the shameful deeds that Hitler's men had done.

Death caught up with my father when he was eighty-two,
He never let me know if he felt pain.
He still could recite Shakespeare the way he used to do
Until the cancer ate away his brain.
I like to think he's met up with his comrades
Who went before him on the last great flight.
I hope they laugh as they recall old glories,
They fought for what they all believed was right,
He told me of the quality of mercy,
I knew Portia's speech before I learned to pray.
May the King of the Jews and the Prince of Peace give welcome
To an Irish airman coming home to stay.

Clare McAfee

MY DAD

My dad is the one I turn to
When my problems overflow,
He wraps his arms around me
When my life seems full of woe.
He's the one who lends to me
When I am short of cash.
If I need a favour,
He's done it in a flash.
He's the one who tucked me in
And kissed me on the cheek
He's the one who made me strong
When I was feeling weak.
He's my pick-me-up when I feel down
When I'm sad he is my clown.
I love my dad and he knows
My love for him just grows and grows.

Rachel Hamlet

POEM FOR DAD - MY FATHER OF THIS EARTH

My dad when I think of you I am so sad
Lots of things I can say now I could not as a lad
You see me now dad and of you I am so sad
Yes I did things that made you mad
You see me now dad why I am so sad
But I am now a man dad like you a father I had
You see me now dad why I am so sad
I am happy when I hear you talk dad yes and glad
You see me now dad a man not a lad

Robert John Quinlan

MY DAD

Who was always there for me
When I fell down or cut my knee
Who would bind it patiently
My Dad

Even when the day was done
and I was worried about doing sums
Who explained them every one
My Dad

Then a gangly teenager
With many hopes and many fears
Who would wipe away my tears
My Dad

When I emerged then as a bride
Who stood with me - flushed with pride
Who was right there by my side
My Dad

Even now - though fully grown
I always know I'm not alone
Who is always back at home
My Dad

The backbone of our family
Guess it isn't hard to see
Who means all the world to me
My Dad

Elizabeth Beckinsale

DAD

I was your first born,
treated like a little princess
spoiled and loved in every way
sometimes, I think, to excess.
I loved you much more
than I ever knew
A child protected by you.
When times were hard
we shared the burdens,
carried each other
through times uncertain.
I clung to you
like a vine to a tree
you struggled too hard
I was too blind to see.
But a child I was
with lack of foresight
As a woman, now I see your plight
how life was such a fight.
You left me, to live on a higher plain
I prayed for you
but all in vain.
As a child I was lost
when you went away
I know if you could
you would come back today.
But I do believe God had work for you
you were an angel on earth
good and true,
Dad, I will always love you.

Jacquie Williams

MODESTY ITSELF

Debonair, salubrious,
Ostentatious and suave
Sophisticated, symmetrical
And too witty to starve.

These are the names
That he calls himself
With a sun-tanned complexion
He's a picture of health

He's sure that he's perfect
In that he will revel
What he sees in the mirror
Is a 'handsome young devil'.

He pulls the kids legs
And they're really not sure
Till his face fills with laughter
And he lets out a roar

When he drives in his car
He owns all the road
And he beeps and he moans
Just like Mr Toad

You can tell from this poem
That he's really quite mad
But I never would change him
He's one unique Dad

Shirley Lidbetter

EIGHT DAYS IN A WEEK

Someday when I have the time I promised myself
I would put down my memories on paper to display on a shelf.
But even now my bookshelf isn't quite complete
As my time is so precious with two children under my feet.
Yet I manage to spare a thought for you as I go through my day
The very little time I give to you when I visit, and even then
                                    I've nothing really to say
I eat your omelette because it's you who have made it for me
It may be made out of eggs but love is the extra ingredient in your recipe.
I sit at your table watching, sometimes your eyes catch mine
A far off different week is recaptured for a moment, as I watch
                                      your eyes shine
A time when you were the axis on which my tiny world would revolve
In a time when I thought you could swim, when there were no
                                problems I had to solve.
In this, my world, it was built in a week but not by God
But by a force who builds with love and doesn't rule with a rod.
A world filled with Thursdays which meant pocket money with
                                   fish and chips too.
All brought home by a special carrier, that person was you.
Taken out in a lorry on a special Sunday in May
We broke down by the quarry which made it a special birthday.
Rugby matches on Saturdays, watched through the bottom of a
                                   pop filled glass.
As I sat upon the Rugby Club's bar far more comfortable than
                                  the packed green grass
As the days passed, on Mondays I borrowed money for my bus fare
                                  to and from work,
Tuesdays I repaid my debt, Wednesdays you handed it back with
                                  a knowing smirk.
On Fridays you'd be waiting outside my school gate
I'd panic if I couldn't see you, or if you were late.
My week has passed so quickly where my world was made
My structure is held together with love, cemented to the foundations
                                  you selflessly laid.
I want there to be an eighth day in my week, which no one else can share.

A special 'Dad's Day' where my time will be yours, to show you
how much I care.
Time is precious, just like you are to me
I love you deeply dad, you can swim in my eyes and not
just in the sea.

Karren Kinsey

DEAR DAD

We used to see the sunshine on the hills,
And could ignore the blight of winter chills.
And all of sadness seemed a distant thing
When gladness caused the whole wide world to sing.

We watched the tiny seedling leaves unfold
And gloried in the dew which made the pearl,
But most of all we loved togetherness,
Each with the same thoughts, no need to guess.

We'd spent a long, long time apart, too long,
Each wandering single through the careless throng.
What was this unseen cord that first did draw
Two people to pursue the road they lately saw?

So wide and even, clearly marked and gay
That they could go together on their way?
We didn't know, nor did we really care,
The path we followed was so good and fair.

And then you left me, not because you chose,
We'd tried to leave the thorn and grasp the rose,
But you'd grown weary with the passing years,
You left, and I had only endless tears.

Joyce M Nicholson

DAD

Ever since I was small, you've provided for me,
always bringing in money for the family,
I've never gone without, there's always been plenty to eat,
and when times have been flush you've given me a treat.

Now you're 52, you still work as hard as ever,
out on the land in any kind of weather,
working on your tractor I know it means everything to you,
and you mean the world to me, Dad, I love you.

Claire J Young

JOHN HARRY - MY DAD

As he walked down the street,
No one blinked an eye,
He was just another little guy,
To every other passer-by.

But to me he was ten feet tall,
Just the greatest dad of all,
He understood when days were grey,
And confusion and doubt came my way.

Then came the day he passed away,
He went to join my mum to stay,
I could not go to say goodbye,
The winter's snow was six feet high.

My dad was such a wondrous pal,
His memory still lives even now,
To me he'll never be history,
Each day he walks and talks to me.

Barbara Duck

MY DAD

They were happy times when I was young
My dad was always full of fun
Although he wished I'd been a boy
I know I was his pride and joy,
For he took me everywhere he could
To play tennis and watch football if I was good,
But one thing we really liked to do
I'd play piano and he'd play Saxophone, clarinet and violin too,
At Christmas time we had great parties
Dad was always first to get the fun started
Games we'd play what fun we'd have
Dad was always game for a laugh,
Oh what happy times we had
I'm sure lucky to have had my dad,
Although he died when I was young
Your praises always will be sung
If everyone had a dad like me
What a lovely place the world would be.

Chris Gardner

TO A VERY DEAR PARENT

My daddy worked so very hard for all of us
He worked shifts and at home with guests and no fuss.
During the war he did home guard duties as well as his work.
Although he was tired his family commitments he did not shirk.

There were three of us children and a mum.
When daddy came home he was such fun.
The help and guidance and love he gave to us.
He went about and everyone looked up to him, he didn't fuss.

M P Morrey

BETTER THE DEVIL

My father slipped back from Valhalla,
And wanted to know what he'd missed,
So we sat on his favourite old sofa,
And I gave him a little list.

I told him we had Karaoke,
And that Torvill and Dean were back,
And that Britain belonged to Europe,
And there's ecstasy, poppers and crack.

I spoke of the National Lottery,
Of the Fax, and those mobile phones,
Of our car boot sales on a Sunday,
Of Jacuzzis, and motorway cones

Of car alarms, Virgin and condoms,
Of Sky and our pub with its quiz,
Of health farms, and Royal divorces,
Of wheel-clamps and Eurodiz.

I think that I've heard all I want to,
Said my dad as he put on his hat,
Since I died I've been living in Hell, but
Believe me - it's better than that!

Peter Davies

DAD

Dad you worked so very hard
Just to make ends meet
Times were hard when I was young
The war was at its end
Ration books little food to eat
No decent shoes upon our feet

You were our leading light
Someone who showed the way
Always there when things went wrong
To lend a helping hand
You wiped away a tear or two
And seemed to understand

Our childhood and our teenage years you shared
With tender love and care
Now you have sadly left us
And life is not the same
But you left behind fond memories
That will never fade away

Gillian Morrisey

DARDANELLES

My father was a soldier in the first world war
His previous job was cooking he had never fought before
When he went to Turkey his lovely hair was black
But after all the slaughter it was white when he came back

He landed on that awful shore from the SS River Clyde
And all around was bloodshed as men fell at his side
With dysentery and wounded he suffered all his life
But that man made a home for twelve kids and a wife

So now dad that I'm eighty and realise what you did
You always were a hero when I was just a kid
You did your best to make us men and a lady of each girl
And everyone's a credit as the passing years unfurl

So cheers dad to your memory which goes forever on
Those days with you and mother will never once be gone
You left us all behind you, one day we'll meet again
But meanwhile we still see you as we look down memory lane.

George Dragon

OUR DAD

I guess we all have
Memories to hold
Of our youth
And of Dad of the stories he told
The way he could play
The piano with ease
He would liven up parties
His aim was to please
He was always so proud
Of my brothers and me
Would tell anyone near
Bend their ears constantly
We will always remember him
Time will never change that
He was so full of life
Never bored I think back
We would go fishing
In his little boat
Fall asleep coming back
There were his funny jokes
We would laugh just to please him
How we loved him so
A dad to be proud of
Though the years come and go

Jeanette Gaffney

MY LOVING DAD

My own dad is dead,
But I have a friend who acts like one instead.
I know I drive him mad
this makes him rather sad.
But I know he's a close friend to me a loving dad.

42

I know he means well
His feelings are easy to tell.
But he's a great guy, swell,
I see him as a dad
this makes me rather glad.
But if it wasn't for him I think I would have gone mad.
I love my loving dad.

James R B McCurdie

AN ODE TO DADS

Dads are short, dads are tall,
Dads like snooker and football,
Dads wear cardigans and smoke pipes,
Dads are all assorted types.

Dads make speeches on your wedding day,
Dads are bald or dads are grey,
Dads drive slowly in the car,
Dads buy you cocktails at the bar.

Dads dig the garden and grow nice flowers,
Dads remember the good old days and talk for hours and hours,
Dads read the papers and keep up with the news,
Dads don't like your music or your trendy shoes.

Dads have pot bellies but some dads are thin,
Dads have patience to teach you how to swim,
Dads don't like to iron or wipe the dust from the shelf,
I should know because you see I've got a dad myself!

Tracy Benjafield

MY DAD
(To Sylvia, my wife, my life)

When I grow up I want to be, like my old dad
He's loving, gentle and kind, but certainly no cad
He can be strict, but we know he's right
But he's still generous with his love, when money's tight
you can see he loves my mum as well
She often says he's swell
He always seems to be happy
And he's never snappy
If I can grow up just like him, that would be great
Loving sincere and loving, so it's you dad I emulate
I know we cause you trouble with our different way of life
But you guide me as I grow, so I try not to bring you strife
But I say this, you would take some beating as a father
I love you for all you're worth, and I could go farther
I put you on a pedestal
And I just know you will never fall
A sharp word keeps me on my toes
And a stern look says he knows
For was not once just like me, many years ago
And I thing granddad took you in tow
But I rate you next to God
Handsome, strong, and if needs be did not spare the rod
I suppose it's because I love you so much
I think you've got the right touch
If I can be just as half as good as you
I will know I've emulated you too
Some might say I brag about you as well
So what, from your son dad, I think you're swell.

Prince Rhan of Kathari

THE BOY FROM MAYO

You broke those chains that bound you
travelled many a road
you were young, strong and eager then
to find those streets of gold
your generosity held no bounds
your knowledge all would seek
those tales of far off yesterdays
we sat spellbound as you'd speak
you would drink your glass of porter
and sip that clear mountain dew
you would sing the saddest ballads
no one sang those songs like you

No crooked road did we take
your words of anger were for our sake
you worked so hard from dawn till dusk
with five of us you knew you must
you fought many a battle
sustained deep wounds no eyes could see
you were young, strong and eager then
I was blind . . . I could not see

But all too soon we have grown
and one by one left you and home
and as you laid in that bed surrounded by strangers
no one there to hold your hand
you travelled that last lonely journey
to heaven, God's promised land
so I raise my glass in memory
for your memory I will always keep
God Bless the boy from Mayo
and those you left behind to weep

V Stott

OH MEIN PAPA

I remember my dear old dad
The Lord grant, that he may sleep in peace.
A lifelong poor man - he couldn't afford
So we rented a house, on a lease.

A firm believer in democracy
he extolled the red, white and blue,
During Britain's darkest hour in 1940
His favourite topic was - the exploits of the 'The Few'.

I remember you well, my father
Along the river banks, we had our evening walks
In my youth, you answered my silly boyhood questions
And later, we had our man to man talks.

How you worried, when I joined the Forces
Was I getting enough to eat?
And each time, I came home on leave
Surreptitiously, you tried to pass me, your small ration of meat.

Yes - I remember you well - my father
My memory of you will never fade,
How, I unashamedly cried, when I heard
That you were the victim of an enemy air raid.

Paul Gold

MY DAD

Gentle and kind with a heart of gold
Not a word of reproach would you hear
For the cruel, painful illness he carried alone
Yet he still knelt each night in prayer.

As a child I recall, I would sit on his knee
And hear stories of Kings and Queens
With fairy tale castles where a Princess lived
A place to remember in dreams.

Picnics in forests with hide and seek
And all the seaside fun.
Sandcastles built especially for me
To knock down one by one.

A happy childhood, truly blessed
By a special dad, now safe at rest.
Secure in his love which has helped me in life
To enjoy my own family - loving mother and wife.

Cynthia Shum

MY DAD

My dad is
funny
not tight with money,
witty,
He'll always sing a ditty.
Caring,
always sharing,
elusive,
persuasive,
young at heart,
slim like a dart,
cheeky,
never a nosy beeky,
sensitive,
informative,
an intellectual
Mr fetch-u-all
Who in the end,
is my best friend.

Joanne Clarke (14)

DAD

Dad, I miss you.
Did I tell you how much I care?
I wish that you were here now,
I could tell you again, to make sure.

We had our ups and downs of course,
But you know that better than I.
I always loved you, no matter what,
Then you were taken from me, I wish I knew why?

We had so little time together
You hardly saw my children grow,
My son that you adored so,
And my daughter you did not know.

They missed a lot not knowing you,
For I knew you better than most.
They would have loved you, as I do,
And of their grandfather, they would boast.

Life would be so very different,
If you were here at this moment in time.
To you I could talk about anything,
And you would always make everything fine.

We shared some special moments
In the short time we had together,
We were two of a kind, you and I
In a father, I could not have wanted better.

It hurts that you are not here now,
And the pain is with me still.
I have to be sure you know dad,
That I love you and always will.

Maureen Gard

DEAR DADDY

Dear Daddy, three years have passed tonight
Since the battle ended, you gave up the fight.
From six foot three, energetic and alive,
They sapped your body and mind, you couldn't survive.
Only 76 years old, it wasn't fair
In this day and age you should still be here.
You worked so hard all of your life
And gave love to me and your wife.
You never made any fuss at the end,
I think of you often; I miss you, my friend.
You supported, encouraged and pointed the way
For all that I might have achieved today.
We had our ups and downs, I know
Our tempers flared and we came to blows
The trouble was, we were rather the same
But my Celtic blood usually caused the flame.
You calmly smoked your pipe and forgave.
I still feel your presence, from the grave.

Jane Uff

A GRAND DAD

Dear Dad - what did you mean to me?
A bedtime story on your knee,
Going fishing on the lake,
Gardening with a hoe and rake,
Happy picnics on the sand,
Cliff-top walks, holding your hand,
Playing endless games of Snap,
Guiding me through each mishap,
Always there to lend a hand,
Thank you Dad - you were real grand!

Sylvia Cooke

A THANK YOU LONG OVERDUE

Thank you for the time you gave,
The day trips out and the holidays,
The clothes I wore, the treats I had,
The patience needed to be my dad.

Thank you for my lovely pram,
The things that made me what I am,
The books, the dolls, my first flower seeds,
The bike, and all my teenage needs.

I know that money was often tight
But you made sure I was all right.
I never wanted, always knew
You'd take care of me as I grew.

Now that so much time has passed
I have the chance to say at last,
Thank you dad for all those years
You made me laugh and dried my tears.

For all the hugs, the love and care,
The memories that we both share.
I tell you now that I'm so glad
God chose you to be my dad.

Elizabeth Read

A TRIBUTE TO DAD

You were always funny and kind
ready each day to help us
whenever we called you, you would find
time to listen and share our trust

We have missed your cheery smile
and often have called your name,
but after reminiscing awhile
our thoughts are always the same.

We could not have had a better dad
I know everyone will agree
he would not want us to be sad
so this must not be his obituary.

It has to sound cheerful and bright
not a dirge said too solemnly
he would have us do what is right
drink a toast, then move on cheerfully.

Jo Parsonson

DAD

Your life it has been very hard for you,
and yet you've managed and always smiled through.
When young and only in your prime,
we could have lost you during war time.
But God I think had your life planned,
he watched over you, and gave a helping hand.
For you are such a special man,
and therefore God set you a special plan.

He planned one day a father you'd be
not an easy task to set a man you see.
Thousands of men have played this role,
and done a very good job I've been told.
But none could hold a candle to you,
to put up with me, and all you've been through.
And so I'd like for you to know,
how dear you are, and how I love you so.
And I thank God daily, and am ever so glad,
that he chose you to be my *Dad.*

Grace Thompson

MEMORIES OF DAD

I remember very well
the good times that I had,
being spoiled and petted
by my beloved dad.

He'd sit me on his knee
when bedtime came along,
and sing me off to sleep.
Oh! How I loved those songs

I seemed to steal the show once
when I danced in Pantomime
As the audience applauded
Dad cried 'that little girl is mine'.

I had a serious illness,
and I'd wake up in the night.
Dad was always there somehow
to make me feel all right.

When I passed to the high school
he was so proud of me.
He worked long extra hours
so he could pay the fee.

Before he had reached fifty
his illness came to stay.
It lasted years and years
until it wasted him away.

I grieved for him for ages
I was so very sad
But now my memories shine so bright
of my beloved dad.

Vera Seddon

WILD BOY

Dad likes to ride his motorbikes,
Wild and fast and free,
Just the way he likes his woman,
But we'll keep that between you and me.

He loves to ride upon two wheels,
And feel that sense of power,
In full control of a raging beast,
Whether sun, hail or shower.

Now my dad's a bit of a wild boy,
When he's sat astride his bike,
He's my dad and I love him,
As much as he loves his bikes.

Julie Thompson

IN MY FATHER'S EYE

What is more beautiful in all the world
Than a new born babe in mother's arms held ?
What is more breathless than any sight
Than a sun setting, ready for night?
What is more passionate, more touching than song
Than to see a man cry when all is wrong?
What is more heartbreaking than that cry
When that man is your father asking why?
What is more touching than that song
When seeing him shattered, his spirit gone?
What is more breathless, more beautiful than all
When he's crying for help and your name he does call?
What once stood before me so strong , so proud
Was now cowered amongst the rest of the crowd
For she's gone, so has he, as I look in his eye
I see that man has now passed him by.

Jaqueline Griffiths

DAYS OF GOLD

My dad tells stories of his life and childhood
About the countryside, wildlife and local wood
How black rabbits were released into the wild
On a nearby hillside when he was a child
These rabbits lived happily and made their home
To this day still these black rabbits do roam
The handful of bees he grabbed on his way to school
They sat, then all stung at once - how cruel!
My dad left school and worked with the plough
Steam engines, splicing ropes, he learned how
Early rising, then a long working day
But how he enjoyed it, he will say
From ploughing fields he worked on the road
With a steam roller and its heavy load
Heathrow Airport, Winchester by-pass he'll say
Are two of the big places he helped lay
His love of countryside and steam live with him now
With his scale model engine and its plough
He travels to steam fairs near and far
With his old caravan and trusty old car
My dad's in his eighties and gives such joy
With tales of when he was just a boy
The pleasure he gives with his stories of old
My dear dad's a gem - pure gold.

Mary Loader

HEY DAD

Hey dad let me tell you
How much you mean to me
Now that I've told you
Do you really see.

Hey dad let me tell you
How much I care
And how much I worry
If you aren't there.

Hey dad let me tell you
You're important to me
And for a long time yet
You I want to see.

Keith L Powell

MEMORIES OF MY FATHER SAMUEL JOHN STINTON

My father went off to war fit and fine and brown
He was demobbed with TB it really got him down.
He went to sanatoriums where they thought cold cured all ills
Doors and windows open wide, while sporting icicles.

I used to go and visit him, to stand beside his bed
Each time I walked into the ward, someone else was dead.
It was a long and lonely fight my father fought with that TB
Thereafter years of treatment he returned home to his family

He'd fought hard for his country wore his uniform with pride
But 'cos he contacted that TB it took him cruel years to die
TB was a killer, death its second name
Tuberculosis struck down families time and time again.

My father was a well-read man, intellectual, people would say
The things he always told me stay with me to this day
I miss my father sorely he stays with me in my mind
A handsome man, Italian looking and very very kind.

He grew up with four brothers, as lads they camped by the Wye.
He told of their adventures, I listened open-eyed.
As father led me up the aisle he turned to me to smile.
Tho' he's gone now, which makes me sad, I am proud he was my dad.

Rita Hughes-Rowland

MAIN INGREDIENT; DAD!

The omelettes I mix;
the bread that I bake
just cannot lick
those that Dad used to make!

Dad's omelettes were sublime;
his pork chops - mm - just great!
All so perfect, every time,
well worth a patient wait.

Bacon pudding was a treat;
soda-bread nice and quick.
Dad's curried mince, I loved to eat:
Nostalgic tastes, in my memory stick!

There was something about Dad's fried bread,
that made it simply melt;
but, served with a simple fried egg -
to me, was like a banquet!

Hot lemonade on a cold winter's morn;
lemon juice on pancakes sweet.
I wish I could taste them all again
when I sit down, *these* days, to eat!

I'll never have the magic touch
of my Dad's cooking skills.
But I'll remember, very much,
those tastes which cured all ills!

But I am so glad
that I was blessed,
with my loving Dad
who cooked the best!

Rosemary A V Sygrave

FOR DAD

For all the love you showed me as a little girl
Thank you Dad
For the tandem and sidecar era
I was so thrilled Dad
When I needed a bike you made one for me
What can I say Dad?
For watching you struggle with little money to spare
My heart is full Dad
For your strength and never being afraid
I'm proud to be your daughter Dad
For showing humanity when you helped to bring your injured friends out
From a pit explosion
I cried with you Dad
For helping me with my homework and never losing patience
A dad in a million
For walking me down the aisle and soothing jangled nerves
Bless you Dad
For being wise when troubles came
A rock to hold fast to Dad
For giving me the strength of your love to help me cope now that you are
Not here
God keep you Dad
I will always love you
Your daughter

Julia Haywood

IN LOVING MEMORY

Dear Dad,
It's been fifteen years since we last spoke - almost to the day -
when you slipped unobtrusively, but painfully away.
I was too late by ten minutes to say a proper goodbye.
At first I felt nothing but relief that you'd been spared
more pain - your once strong body reduced to a skeletal shadow,
with yellowing skin, and flesh pared almost to the bone.
For your last meal I fed you strawberries
through teeth too large for cancer-shrunk lips.
The following day I sat in your chair,
listened to your music from your much-prized collection -
Handel's 'Hallelujah Chorus', and Beethoven's 'Der Geist' -
They seemed an appropriate choice somehow . . .
Long ago in my teenage years we had little in common,
but music gradually became an enjoyment that joined our minds,
along with the correct employment and rhythm of words;
these things drawing us closer to each other . . .
And the memory of that closeness then caused angry tears to flow;
anger and grief that I had never really sought to know
you better. Your granddaughter - your 'little princess' -
gained her degree in Theology two years ago;
and you have a grandson, conceived the night you died -
a sport fanatic, like yourself,
(although his taste in music would deeply offend
your sense of order and harmony) . . .
But in all other respects you would have been good friends.
I guess there's no more news - nothing else to be said,
except once more, Goodbye, sleep well, and until we meet again -
Godbless. All my love; your daughter, Jen.

J Margaret Service

THE FAILURE

I remember this place where we stopped,
my father and I, a child, on country walks.

He tapped on the gate with his stick
and hundreds of rabbits raced,
in a rushing wave of white,
over the field.

He taught me much about nature,
the Warwickshire scene;
bird song, wild flowers, the shapes of trees,
creatures of woods and streams.

At home he read to me; often beyond my grasp.
Once: 'Tell me where is Fancy bred?'
Thinking it *his* question
I visualised the loaves of magic shape.
'At the baker's shop,' I said.
(He explained 'Fancy'.)

His interest never failed me, nor his love,
which bolstered me throughout a long career.
Unfailing, he was always there for me;
when I'd left home, he still was always there.

Remembering how I failed *him* at the last, I grieve.
Reading to him on visits, he being blind
in later years, was not enough.
He wanted me there to stay,
to be with him there, to stay,
and I failed him then, I failed.

Geraldine Squires

MY DAD

My dad was a wonder to behold,
And many a tale he had wondrously told,
About his adventures during the war,
Coming home disabled when work was poor.
He cobbled shoes to make ends meet,
On top of a clerical job so we would have a treat.
A man so skilled he would make and mend things,
And turning wood for children's enjoyment he would bring.
He could draw and paint also sew a fine seam,
Unusual in a man to create was his dream.
He sat for hours to help us learn,
With a smile on his face and never was stern.
He kept a world of knowledge up in his head,
And did crossword puzzles and was so well read.
He would whistle a tune and watch people dance,
And everything we did his approval he enhanced.
On crutches he did amble for fifty odd years,
Always so happy and never with a tear.
He made many friends and not one enemy did he have,
As he always had good to say and nothing bad.
When he died we were at a great loss,
For the dad was our friend and not a boss.
He will always be cherished for a thousand and one things,
But most of all was the love to everyone he did bring.

Valerie Marshall

FATHER, DEAR FATHER

Father was a gardener, for him all things would grow
He was forever busy with his fork, or rake, or hoe.
His days were filled with labour as he turned the rich, black soil
He'd calluses upon his hands, a back bent from honest toil.

60

He didn't use machinery, he did it all by hand
He didn't earn a fortune but he was happy on the land
No matter what the weather a job he always found
There were seedlings to be raised then planted in the ground

And when the harvest time came round and everything was stored
Then he'd look round with satisfaction, he asked for no reward
Just to know that he'd provided food for all the family
He was a really lovely man, there was no finer dad than he.

Elizabeth Cook

A DAD'S LOVE

Love was a special between my dad and me
There was no pretend it just flowed free

It was always waiting there
Displaying all that loving care

With never a groan or grumble
When I did stray or stumble

But this was in the long-since past
I'm sorry it did not forever last

For God took him way home
Gently called his name to come

The hurt I got was hard to bear
But with others I can now share

A dad's love that knew no limit
Is one thing I'd love to inherit

If you still have a loving dad
Cherish him don't make him sad

Then in the future if like me you be
Fondest memories are yours for free

Maureen Dawson

I'M JUST AN ORDINARY MAN

I'm just an ordinary man, but

That's my *Dad* that is . . .

I sit at my desk at night, working so very hard
To give my children the very best that I can give
And I'm reminded of my *Dad* because,

That's my *Dad* that is . . .

My daughter says to me with an incomprehensible admiration,
'*Dad,* you're the best, why are you so good at drawing?'
And she reminds me of me.
And I tell her,

That's my *Dad* that is . . .

And my son listens to me sing or play a simple tune on the guitar,
And thinks that I should be on the stage
And I remember the time,
When I stood as part of a crowd of true appreciators,
And heard said, 'That man's incredible, the drummer's a king'
And a little boy told them,

That's my *Dad* that is . . .

Of every gentle moment to encourage or console,
And for all the goodness and rare moments of wisdom
That I am capable of and my children benefit from,

That's my *Dad* that is . . .

You see *Dad*, my children see in me something special, something rare,
With a pride that I know so very well.
But the greatness is yours not mine,
The only easy way I can define, is that,
I'm just an ordinary man, but,

That's my *Dad* that is . . .

Adrian Jenkins

DADDY WILL BE PLEASED

Daddy will be pleased with me, he said his petrol's low.
He left the car at home today; I thought I'd help and so
I went into the garage and undid the petrol cap,
Then I put a hose inside and fixed it to the tap.
I couldn't see inside the tank and wondered when to stop.
It took lots and lots of water though to fill it to the top.

Daddy will be pleased with me, I've helped all on my own.
I heard him telling mummy that the fishpond's overgrown.
Lots of choking waterweed, too much for me to dig,
So I found a can of 'Killitall'. The can was really big!
I poured it in the fishpond and I used up every drop.
The goldfish are so happy they're all floating on the top!

Daddy will be pleased with me, last night I heard him say
'They should clean up television.' When he'd watched a silly play.
I couldn't understand at first, it looked alright to me.
All nice and shiny polished bits were all that I could see.
But when I took the back off it was full of dust and fluff,
So I washed it out with water. I hope it's clean enough!

Daddy will be pleased with me, he's always working hard,
Tidying the garden shed and cleaning up the yard.
He spent hours in the garden with a spade and rake and hoe
Planting lots of beans and things and hoping that they'd grow.
But I could see that there would be no chance for daddy's seeds
Until I got his spade and dug up rows and rows of weeds.

Daddy will be pleased with me, he said he didn't know
How many pictures he had taken at the motor show.
So when I found his camera, whilst looking for my ball,
I looked inside and found there were no pictures there at all!
I love to help my daddy, I feel so good somehow.
Oh, goody goody gumdrops, here comes daddy now!

Dennis Turner

MY DAD

I had a very precious dad
A gentle-man was he.
When he'd relax at end of day
I'd sit upon his knee.
Sometimes he'd play the organ,
Sometimes piano he.
But he would sing so very loud
And in chorus include me.
My dad he worked so very hard
Sometimes so far from home
He'd tell the mysteries of the sea,
The dangers of the roads,
He'd paint me pictures
Crowded towns or city lights,
But one thing I shall treasure
Long walks on clement nights
By parks and lanes to harbour pier,
We'd view the yachts and rigging here,
Then turn again for home.
But now - I'm glad I have his nose,
His chin, his fingers and his toes
This lovely man, called Dad.

Jean Devoy

MAN OF MANY TALENTS

So multiple the talents within this man so dear
From musical appreciation to DIY and more;
The outdoor life brought him joy, a spade, a rake, a hoe
Time was spent so lovingly, to work and turn the soil.

Hours were spent out walking, the windy roads of old
Sure just round every corner, a turning point was to be;
The dog his true companion at his heel he walked along
Just like we, the offspring of this very special man

A company accountant is what he was, his work he had to do
My daddy just like other folk had a living to secure;
But when night came and dinner done, relax, unwind he did
With all of us around him, the ivory keys he played.

The weekends flew for all of us no idle moments then
Assistants and apprentices to many trades we were;
Sure from papering and painting, and many other tasks
Sure my daddy and we his work mates, enjoyed each moment then.

Catherine O'Kane

MY DAD

My Dad, my star, my mentor.
He taught me all I know,
About how I should live my life.
How to do things he did show.
He gave me strength to live life
And the confidence to try.
A moral code of conduct
For me to live life by.
He taught me how to love and care
And do my best for others.
That children need a father's love
As much as they need mother's.
He taught me to be caring
But also to be bold.
To always challenge what I heard
Not believe all I am told.
My Dad made me who I am
I tried to be like him.
And though he's been dead for many years
I still feel close to him.

Valerie Lloyd

FATHERS AND SONS

Father dear Father, what trauma you face
Now that you've seen your new son join our race
His presence consumes you, with feelings so strong
Surely possessiveness can't be so wrong!
A being so helpless, no answer has he
When with his small body you make yourself free
His nappy wants changing, his bottle is due
And who will attend to these duties but you?
Your wife is so grateful, she lets you take charge
Take over his life, and his all, by and large.
He loves you, confirms it with chuckle and smile
You are his hero, it stands out a mile!
You lift him to hug him, too young to protest
No thought for the day he'll be leaving the nest
His playmates are vetted, through toddler to teens
And that's when it's threatening quarrels and scenes
He wants to hang out with a gang you don't like
You seriously view confiscating his bike
'You think me a baby, I'm not anymore
Much more of this, and I'll walk out the door!'
A chill grips your heart and you ponder anew
'Am I making mistakes?' To be frank just a few!
He isn't your property, body and soul
As nanny you've more than completed your role
Remember our children to us only lent
To own them for life, well, it just wasn't meant
So slacken the reins, to be comrade *and* Dad
You'll get his respect, and considered 'not bad'!
Just roll back the years, and remember the days
When *your* Dad did his damndest to alter *your* ways!

Doris Holland

THE MEMOIRS OF YESTER YEAR

My childhood years I recall with pride.
The ups and downs of life Dad took in his stride.
Leisurely he took time to light his pipe.
All the time in the world you'd think was his right.

Time meant nothing to him in those days.
Relaxed he taught us right from wrong.
As I reached adolescence I was often amazed.
How he read the newspaper digesting each page.

The local news in the paper discussed with Mum.
As she made garments for my sister and me.
School homework supervised by Dad until all was done.
Then to play, or to and fro from a swing on the tree.

Long winter nights, story telling or singing of songs.
Kept us amused so the nights didn't seem long.
Friends would call in for advice or a chat.
Mum gave them tea and apple tart.

Some wintry morns Dad, horse and cart.
A trailer full of pigs he would head for the Mart.
Home from school annoyed we would be.
If Dad wasn't home and the time half past three.

In the distance for at least half a mile.
We could hear the patter of horses' feet.
Dad would soon reach home and would give us a smile.
And no doubt he would always bring us a treat.

A legacy of honesty and truth was ours to maintain.
Dishonesty and lies would have caused him great pain.
Dad handed down his belief for us to sustain.
I thank you Dad if I err I am to blame.

Putting others first was always a must.
Honouring our parents in whom we did trust.

Elizabeth Swaile

UPON YOUR BIKE

Upon a chilled, red-tiled doorstep -
A tousled child stood and leapt,
Listening out for factory hoot -
Ears pricked for the sound,
Watching on the stroke of five -
For workers homeward bound.

Glancing down the narrow street -
Awaiting for a tea-time treat,
For Dad upon the polished seat of his bike -
I'd run to greet.

Though weary in his boiler suit -
Wi' solder sparkling on his boots,
Grime and grease smeared on his face -
He'd lift me up to take my place -
Upon his crossbar holding tight -
To handlebars wi' all me might!

We glided around the huddled streets -
His legs a-pumping down his feet,
To pedal turn the oily chain -
Round and round and round again!

Come rain or wind, come snow or sun -
This was danger! This was fun!
I was me father's daring son -
Another race and trophy won!

With ring-o-bell, with shouts and cheers
Flicking 'Sturmey-archer' gears,
Switching headlamp off and on -
Until wi' brakes and skidding heels -
We stopped in squeal o' wobble wheels!

Into the parlour went his bike -
Into my heart each memory,
Of Dad who cared enough to spare -
The time to make a young lad's day -
Upon his bike to ride at play.

Philip Joseph Mee

UNTOLD FEELINGS

Seven years ago he came to stay,
A Step Dad to replace the father who went away.
A boy of eight and a girl of fifteen
Who never before had this man seen.
He took us in as if we were his own
And created a family and a happy home.
Once again we saw mum smile
Something we had not seen for quite a while.
New to each other, dubious to start
But he soon crept in to all our hearts.
He played the role of a doting dad
He is the father we never had.
He shows an interest in all we do
And when we stumble he pulls us through.
Hard going at times though it may have been
He is the King and treats our mother like a Queen.
Together they teach us right and wrong
And tell us to walk proud and be strong.
We may not always show we care
But Allan I am glad you are always there.
I'm sorry for our ups and downs
Forgive me if I made you look upon me with a frown.
You are the best father I have ever had
And I do really consider you as my Dad.

Angeline J Joffe

ME DAD

Me Dad, he never wears a cap,
He thinks he is above all that,
A tiny hat he wears instead,
And as he puts it on his head,
Into the mirror, you'll hear him say,
'Man, you're lookin' well today!'

An eccentric man is he, you'd say,
Always goes his own sweet way,
Stands on the corner - chants 'Good day,'
As people pass him by and wave.

His working day at seven starts,
He begins the day with groans and barks,
Has a 'Sup o Tay' and off he carts,
To feed the bastes and visit marts.

By ten o'clock, his hunger strikes,
He darts to cafe with all his might,
Has an Ulster Fry which he devours,
That takes up at least two hours.

Then, it's back to farm, to polish brass,
To give his mares a touch of class,
As all around his 'cronies' work,
They polish harness, shovel dirt,
Whilst 'Big Wullie' tells his tales,
Of bygone days (they never fail).

His 'croonies' stand, with open mouths,
'Quahie, quahoe' is what they shout!
With a Dad like this, I'm overjoyed,
Oh, how I wish I was self-employed!

Lee Chidlow

UNSPOKEN LOVE

Have I ever told you Dad
How much you mean to me?
Perhaps I couldn't find the words
To tell you, let you see.

The years have passed, we can't turn back
The clock and start again.
I wish we could, I would have saved you
So much grief and pain.

So many times you made me laugh
When my whole world went wrong
The twinkle in your eye, your smile
I wasn't sad for long.

You always knew the way I felt
Could almost read my mind.
You shared my love, my luck, my tears
From you I could not hide.

The time has gone so quickly
And now I'm much older too.
I hope that I've grown wiser,
If I have, it's down to you.

The wrinkles show, the hair's turned grey
For both of us it seems,
But we still have our memories, can look back,
Relive our dreams.

So thank you Dad, for being there
You made me realise,
Some words need not be spoken
We can read them in our eyes.

Mary Brooke

A SNOWFLAKE FELL FROM HEAVEN

A snowflake fell from Heaven
    And took my dad away
But I still think about him
    Even to this very day
Let me tell you about my dad
    How good he was to me
Helping me through with living
    From when he sat me on his knee
What more could anyone wish
    Than the love of a father's heart
The 'angels' opened up the door
    When my father did depart
We had so much fun together
    How I miss him now he's gone
But still I've got my memories
    And of course life still goes on
Dad if you can hear me
    I promise you're not alone
Wherever you are I love you
    You're still my king upon a throne.

Kelly Lynn

THE MAJOR

John was a soldier of great esteem, zealous too,
Serving his country for many years, loyal and true.
He was awarded the MBE. For what? He wouldn't say,
Nor did he boast, and never disclosed, to his last day.

Neighbours in St Georges, saw his garden grow,
Manure by the cart load, double digging too you know.
Rows and rows of vegetables, you name it, growing there,
You should have seen his onions! A size beyond compare.

Gardening was his forte, he excelled at that,
Spending hours working, he hardly ever sat,
Except to share his produce or natter to a friend.
He never flagged come rain or shine toiling to the end.

We feel privileged to have known you,
Take a well earned rest now - John!
What can we say of such a man, except -
Two words - well done!

Audrey Pincombe

MY WONDERFUL DAD

Riding high upon your shoulders
Such a long way off the ground
But you held me oh so tightly
I knew I was safe and sound.
Playing way down in the cellar
With an oil can and some screws
Me and my little brother
Watched over carefully by you.
Climbing onto your back
While you were on all fours
Trotting round the room, so fast,
You made a smashing horse!
Building up a train track
In the loft, so we could play,
Rigging up toy telephones
For use on rainy days.
I remember all these things
And all the fun we had,
Now they're just special memories
But you're still my wonderful *dad*.

A M Laycock

MY DAD

You're one of the old school
You're worth your weight in gold
They don't make them like you anymore
You're a treasure to have and to hold

You always bring the sunshine
When the rain falls
You're the apple of my eye
You are my good cause

The years they come
The years they go
But you never falter
And I really love you so
Because I'm glad that I'm your daughter

You have shown me the light
You've shown me the right way
You've never stopped showing me
Right up to this day

Whatever I may do
Wherever I may go
I know you'll always be there
I know you'll love me so

You're kind and understanding
With your unselfish love
I know you're always there
I thank the Lord above

Pat Bell

DEAR DAD

Dear dad remember on a Saturday morn
We'd off to the sawmills hastily born
Me up ready and eager to start
You'd push me there in that wooden hand cart
And when we used to go for rides
Both on bikes me close at your side
When I got tired and lagged like a snail
You'd pull me along holding on your coat tail
The Sunday walks to the Fox and Hounds
Me sitting outside 'cos it was out of bounds
A packet of crisps bottle of Vimto too
Those days all gone were all too few
Taking me to the fair at night
Boy it was a wonderful sight
You couldn't win at the coconut shy
So you coax the man a coconut to buy
The day you had me searching the lane
With your funny little money game
You said half crowns were being dropped there
When one in your hand was all that was spare
Lots of old sayings you always had
Right from when you were a lad
Things like 'Hells Bells' and 'Sup Me Bob'
And my leg 'Hurts like Billio' I'd hear you sob
Through your gruffness you showed you cared
But memories Dad we no longer share
Still they're here, they're mine to keep
'Cos I've lost you dad to that long deep sleep

Elizabeth Hurcombe

THE WHISTLING MAN

The streets are still and quiet
And nothing makes a sound,
But something breaks the silence
When the whistling man comes round.

Above a crowd of people
The whistle can be heard,
They all look round expectantly
To see a songful bird.

He whistles in the morning
He whistles late at night,
He whistles in the bathroom
And when it's dull or bright.

The dogs come running to the whistling sound
And taxis brake for fare,
Imagine their amazement
When there's no-one waiting there.

Before we get up from our beds
The whistling man's about,
I try to get up early
But I never catch him out.

You might think he's a milkman
Well than you've just been had,
Coz I know who he really is
The whistling man's my dad!

Carol Prior

IF ONLY
(In memory of my father George Lindsay Crozier)

This poem, is for my father,
The kindest man, I've known.
I never took the time, to say,
How much my love, had grown.
If only, I had used the words,
It would have meant, so much.
To let him know, in some small way,
In his life, our hearts he touched.
It is too late, to tell him,
I wish I could turn back the clock.
To see his warm and gentle smile,
In each memory, time lovingly unlocks.
He is gone but not forgotten,
Like the happy times, we shared,
He was one in a million, a gentleman,
I hope he knew, how much we cared.

Shirley Thompson

DAVID - MY DAD

With his bracers and shorts
With his slippers so old
With his green woolly gown
and his hands draped in gold

A laugh a minute
A helping hand
Someone to turn to
He'll understand

A wonderful life
the best I've had
A wonderful family
and the best dad.

Dawn Louise Bell

YOUNG DARK THOUGHTS

Why do you beat me so much dad
In my silent abyss mind, you're glad.
Every day was a nightmare
Every day a grind and despair,
Born in '31 life's misery began,
Food so scarce, life's humdrum.

Your money spent on vile drink
Tummy doesn't matter, family can sink,
Get to bed, that's what he said,
Hunger pangs I always dread,
The children you bore in this storm,
Better were I dead, yes my mind so torn.

School, the same beating from sisters, their scorn,
I thought a ruler was a measure
But a smack 6 times must give them pleasure
But, but, I ran inside not to get a punch
Harry and co, so tall started the crunch.
A smack in the ear, a punch in the back.

Complain at home? No, I'd be put on the rack
Looking for love from some source or other
Getting none from sisters, brothers, or mother.
I'm sure this life isn't natural
But beatings daily was factual.
When Germany started the war
Dad called up, beatings withdrawn.

Dad is now dead, buried in Bristol,
I'm sure I would be there too, if he'd had a pistol.

Derrick Bright

A LEGACY OF MEMORIES

I've so many lovely memories of a very caring dad.
Who so very willingly shared everything he had.
He worked hard from morn to night, to provide for eight of us.
And though sometimes he looked so tired, he never made a fuss.
He would cut our hair, and mend all our shoes.
Sometimes it was late at night, before he read the news.
During school holidays, we'd have a day by the sea
Taking a picnic basket, and Thermos flasks of tea.
After we'd had our sandwiches, we made castles in the sand
Then we'd wander to the 'prom' to listen to the band.
Sometimes we were lucky, and saw a Punch and Judy show
Which we kids stayed watching, until it was time to go.
Then we were taken home, the end of a perfect day.
We all hoped next holiday, we'd go for a longer stay.
I've a treasure chest of memories, left me by my dad.
They will always remind me, of the happy years we had.

Gladys Cook

OUR DAD

Our dad is no longer alive,
Although our memories of him will always survive.
When we were small he was so much fun,
Took us everywhere with plenty of hols in the sun.
Picnics and parks and games in the dark.
Presents and sweets and lots of treats.
As we grew up with children of our own,
He was still the same, and he never moaned.
He was doting and caring, number 1 in sharing.
He would wait at the gate when children came from school,
With a tin full of toffees or ice pops or lollies.
Our dad was so loving and definitely the best,
Everyone admired him, God bless our dad who's now laid to rest.

Janet E Isherwood

MY DAD

A luckless lad am I
Whose life seemed to pass him by
When the best friend a wish could bring
Was taken away from him.

As a child I wondered why
That when alone my mum would cry
But as time pulled back the curtain
It was then I knew for certain.

That now my dad was just a name
And that death was not a game
It was a cancer that betrayed him
And left two little boys to crave him.

At the age of twenty-nine
A man cut down in his prime
Who was skilled and dedicated
But now killed, not educated.

A figure hardly known yet missed
The top of my most wanted list
The one I dedicate this thought to
My father John - I do still miss you.

Neil Gould

MY DAD

Lucky are they, that have a dad,
I had one once, and I was glad.
I knew him just for a little while -
He had a happy laugh, and made me smile,
My mam took over the job at hand,
And was my mam and dad, the best in the land.
Precious memories were left with me,
So sad it was, my dad drowned at sea.

Sheila MacDonald

MY DAD

Hans Christian Anderson,
Tales of Rupert Bear,
For my bedtime story,
I'd curl up in his chair.

Listening to the wireless,
Sitting on his knee.
Dick Barton, 'special agent'
Was a favourite with me.

His pleasures were so simple,
Listening to the band.
Perhaps a picnic in the park,
Or walking hand in hand.

One day I thought I'd lost him,
From work he was so late.
The factory bombed so badly,
A lifetime I did wait.

With outstretched arms he came,
Tears running down his face.
He had to leave his friend there,
But he was home, and safe.

On my wedding morning,
He was too proud by far.
He jumped out with my bouquet,
And left me in the car.

He was a very quiet man,
Never a 'Jack the lad'
But to me he was so special,
For to me he was *my dad*.

Peggy Howe

OVER THE HILLS AND FAR AWAY
(For Sebastian John Rhodes, flautist, singer,
composer and most importantly, best loved father)

I was only three when I first saw you play
'Over the Hills and Far Away'
Up on that stage, with your black wooden flute,
Silver keys flashing, notes that poured
Liquid and golden - my spirit soared.
My daddy's up there! So proud was I,
I wanted to laugh and dance and cry.

Then as years went by I saw less of you,
Daddy's at work, (and far away)
And the world came in and stole our song;
I wanted to sing, but the music had gone.

In the garden shed you'd sometimes play
In the odd moments you could steal away.
But over the years the music died,
And you didn't explain, and I couldn't know
How hard you worked for us all, just so
We'd have food to eat and shoes on our feet,
And a safe home where we could thrive and grow.

Though I tried to play piano and carry on,
My traitor fingers were clumsy and coarse.
The childhood illness that stole my sense of smell
Seemed to have left me tone deaf as well.

So I'm sorry I couldn't carry on your song,
But it'll never be lost, nor the magic gone
For whenever I hear the notes of a flute
A door inside opens to that golden world
You took me to once, where all joys unfurl;
Where I know you wait, flute in hand,
For me to come and hear you play
'Over the Hills and Far Away'

Felicity Howard

DAD

Dad is a word that's hard to define, everyone's different and they change
                                                                    with time.
Dads can be helpful loving and kind, I think mine is one of a kind.
The reason is simple he's a master of craft, making things without plans
                                                                    or draft.
The original Mr Fixit make good, whether it be in metal or wood.
Always helpful a friend to many, guaranteed to save you more than a penny.
There's nothing he won't attempt to repair, he's even swept chimneys
                                                                    without a care.
If I have a problem I give him a call, he may be older but he's still on the
                                                                    ball.
As time goes by more help he does need, but life's like that we all must
                                                                    take heed.
He enjoys his life at least as he's able, a pint, a bet and food on the table.
He has a wish to make the news, win the lottery and go on a cruise.

A Sackey

DEAR FATHER OF MINE

So you want to know what he meant to me
Dear father of mine
Then - I'll take you back and show you
In the patter of this rhyme
He was silver haired and handsome
A distinguished gentle soul
Full of warmth and love and wisdom
A mind never to grow old.
To him a little girl forever
In his eyes I'd always be
As for me, my rock my tower
Still missed, still loved, still with me.

Pamela Lannon

DAD, I WISH

I wish I'd listened to all the advice, forever flowing
    from your protective mind,
I wish I could know what I know now, and I could
    leave all those wrong turns behind,
And I wish I could travel on your train of thought,
    and see where you'd want to go,
I just wish I could step back in time, and enjoy all
    those childhood memories, that because of you,
                       I know.

I wish your steadying hand would stay on my shoulder,
    comforting me with a pat, when I'm down,
I wish you could hear my dilemmas, when my head spins,
    and my face contorts into a frown,
Most of all, I couldn't wish for a better father, a
    companion, friend, and sole, trustworthy man,
If only death could be scared off, I'd stand forever in
    front of you, with a stick in my hand.

Stephen J Cooper

DADDY'S GIRL

When I was a child maybe seven or eight,
I followed you dad wherever you went,
I sat on your knee or tight in your arms,
Always secure, no worries or qualms.

My teenage years were approaching fast,
You worried dad how long they would last,
When problems loomed and secrets were kept,
Yours was the shoulder on which I wept.

I was the clay and you moulded me so,
You made me stronger and helped me cope,
Now I've grown into an adult myself,
I know how you worried, I know how you felt.

But the pride I feel when you walk by my side,
Has never changed much just grown in size,
From the little girl who adored you so,
To the woman who loves you dad more than you know.

Jill Cockerill

ONE OF THE BEST

A helping hand he'd always give
to people in their need.
An upright straight and honest man,
a gentleman indeed.

Though he was just a countryman
he'd wisdom unsurpassed.
All our problems he would solve,
he could not be outclassed.

He taught me how to stand up straight,
and speak out for what's right.
My inspiration and my guide,
a radiant shining light.

When I look down those golden years,
those memories of time,
I know the best of what I am,
I owe that dad of mine.

Though he's been gone for many a year,
his memory's in my mind.
I pray that when my own time comes,
my dear old dad I'll find.

Fred Wyer

LEGACY OF LOVE

You never left us on our own,
You were always by our side.
Through stressful times your love still shone.
Though your heart was broken inside.

Together we learned to pick up the pieces.
You taught us the need to be strong.
Tenderly you would wipe the tears from our faces.
With gentle guidance - you taught us right from wrong.

We didn't always do things the way that you wanted.
We had ideas and opinions of our own.
Yet you never dictated, nor rules at us flaunted.
There you still were, when we started to moan.

We needed no gifts, to show us you cared.
There are some things that money just can't buy.
You could have left too, but our lives you still shared.
Back then dad, you were one hell of a guy.

You never wanted payment, your love came for free,
At what cost to yourself, I never thought to comprehend.
A price cannot be put on the love you gave to us three.
Many thanks for being there, a father and a friend.

As years roll by we never say, the things we really should,
To those who mean so much, those who have been so good.
I know I don't say it often, and you know I wouldn't lie,
I truly love you heaps dad - you are still one hell of a guy.

Linda Welbourn

THE SEQUINNED PURSE

Daddy, o daddy, o daddy of mine
        Why are you passing away?
I heard your laughter
        On rising, today
Locked fast in my memory
        Through annals of time past
O, why are you passing away?

Leaving me grieving
        Why should you be leaving?
Remembering my childhood,
        The sound of your laughter
Remember the moment in time
        When you stepped off the train, on that day?
Met your daughter, a stranger
        As you came back from danger
O, why are you passing away?

Remember the purse that you gave me
        When you stepped off the train,
Came back from the wars, on that day?
        I was a stranger to you then, remember?
Remember the kisses, the khaki, the kitbags,
        Thrown down on the platform
O, why are you passing away?

The purse, in the sunshine
        All glittering with sequins
Symbolic the gift, that you gave me, that day
        Along with the courage I need for life's journey,
O, why are you passing away?

Joyce Bridle

MY STRENGTH, MY DAD

When thinking of life's wonders
I cast my mind on you
The memories of the happy times
Like the sun, come shining through
You were my strength when needed
You were the light at the end of the gloom
You took away the shadows
That crowded every room
You always see the funny side
Of things when they go wrong
So if I was feeling down at times
I could not feel that way for long
I don't know what I would have done
Had you not been there
To have someone as special
Who I know will always care
You always know the right things to say
You always know what to do
You're a very special person
Dad, I do love you.

Colleen Knight

FOR MY DAD

The awful agony of waiting
Not knowing how you are
The stillness of the night
The semblance of a star.

To be so very close to you
Through all the passing years
And now to know you feel so ill
Just fills my heart with tears.

But you have learned, and so have I
To hold our heads up high,
To hold to life with courage true
So that whatever we may do,
Or ever have to face
Will go on gallantly, fighting still,
His strength and courage in our will.

Jean Humphris

THOUGHTS ON FATHER'S DAY

He only had to look at us
To quell rebellious streak
And if he did admonish us
We didn't dare to speak.
His ways were quite Victorian
A legacy from gran,
He was our stalwart guardian
A moral upright man.
He was of grim demeanour
And very rarely smiled
And yet beneath that stern facade
He was so meek and mild.
The evidence was plain to see
With grandchildren about
His golden times much happier
Of that there is no doubt.
Retirement years with mother
They never seemed to pall
Long working days behind him
We watched his burdens fall.
And when with age and frailty
He reached his journey's end
We hadn't only lost our dad
We'd lost a loving friend.

Marion P Webb

THE BEST

No finer dad could there ever be
I was the third child of a happy family
When I was ever sad or in despair
I would go to dad for advice he was always there.

Ready to listen and give a helping hand
Whatever the problem he would understand
Always with a smile, he would brush away the tears
Gently talk through my troubles and calm my fears.

In my school days he would help me with my homework
Quietly saying try harder and do not shirk
Then at weekends I would go with him on a hike
Or ride pillion passenger on his old motorbike.

No better teacher could I ever have had
Than my caring 'best in the world' dad
He taught me to show compassion for our elders and animals alike
Never to turn my back if I saw them in any plight.

To give a helping hand, to others in need
This was the moral that he taught me to believe.
He would say take nothing for granted and always pay your way
I will remember his words of wisdom until my dying day.

Now the years have passed, and I am woman grown
And I have little children of my own
I will try to teach and give them, the happy childhood that I had
Ever grateful for his patience and love, to the world's best dad.

Brenda Colvin

MY FATHER

My father was a miner
At a tender age he went
Beneath the ground
To cut the coal
To help the family rent

Many dangers he met there
He survived each and all
Until the day
The mine blew up
But he escaped the fall

It was then he decided
He must leave that industry
Once in London
Then back home
In the building industry

In South Wales he settled down
And there met his future wife
Through the hard times
And the good times
He lived an exemplary life

He worked hard, had no vices
And loved his wife and family
He had two boys
And then three girls
All brought up properly

He may not have achieved fame
In the rollcall, but to
His children and
Grandchildren he was
The best father of all

Terence Daley

A STRONG DAD

My dad was a big dad, a kind dad, a good dad, his shoulders were broad
and his arms they were strong.

My dad was a fun dad, a teasing dad, a joking dad, his humour was sharp
and his laughter was long.

My dad was a working dad, an oily dad, an overtime dad,
his boiler suit was filthy, his tractors in a row.

My dad was a strict dad, a glaring dad, a stern dad,
his justice was fair, his forgiveness was sure.

My dad was a reading dad, a cricket dad, a pint dad,
his politics were socialist, his house an open door.

My dad was a Christmas dad, a Santa dad, a stocking dad,
his Christmas dinner cooking, his lighted Christmas star.

My dad was a bow dad, an arrow dad, a stilt dad,
his sledges were the greatest, his go-carts best by far.

My dad was a small dad, a sick dad, a tired dad,
his voice wasn't working, his eyes didn't see

My dad is a big dad, a strong dad, a good dad,
his body's gone to heaven and his spirit waits for me.

Judith Christie

THANK YOU DAD

Thank you dad for all those lifts
Before I found a boyfriend with a car.
And for all the holidays we went on
Some near and some afar.

Those terrible jokes I learnt from you
That make the family groan.
And for letting me bend your ear
Whenever I felt like a moan.

92

We shared a lot of happy times
And a few that were sad.
I just wish, before you passed away
I'd had time to say 'thank you dad'.

E Brenton

MY DEAR FATHER

Dearest father, you were a lovely man
So kind, gentle and generous
The best of all the family clan
But why did you have to suddenly leave us?

Mother and I, were utterly devastated
When you left us in 1965
We wept until our eyes were sore and red
And couldn't believe you weren't still alive

All these years on, we still sorely miss you
And think of you every single day
No matter where we are, or what we do
Our lives in tatters and disarray

You were a clever scholar and academic
Nicknamed the living lexicon
You taught me to appreciate books and music
But I wasn't clever enough to become a don

I know how often you were disappointed in me
Being so dim at school made you feel low
But you were always so tolerant, never angry
And never let the hurt show

One day we're bound to be together again
With so much to tell each other
In a far better and more peaceful domain
Until then, love from mother and me, dear father

Marion Beata Gunnell

DA

Pal of my childhood days, I've needed you always
Since first you held me, upon your knee
You sacrificed everything for me
I never said, nor did you comprehend
How much I loved you then
A father's role, is oftimes overlooked
You gave your all, asked for nothing back.

I remember how expertly, you could farm and fish
Row a boat, weave a basket, reap, thresh
The yellow corn; afterwards I twisted the straw ropes!
Build bricks, stones, solder with cement, yet
Conversed with peers, freely, had their respect.
A person once met, one could not easily forget.
Not scorned, nor ever despised the poor
Never refused them, alms at his door
Everyman's friend, as he was to them.

For me, always ready to mend broken things
His pockets forever seemed to contain
Curious things: nails, glue, sealing wax, pieces of string.
I remember his changing moods; sometimes irate, others mild
Awed and confounded me, as a child.
Alternately he frowned, and smiled.
Long silent lapses, would then ensue.
Dear da, friend, philosopher, and guide, too.

A humble man, with a humane heart.
Ahead of his time; a dreamer of dreams.
Yet deep within, a realist, where contentment reigned.

Hannah Maguire

NATURE'S GENTLEMAN

With Dvorak's 'New World' symphony drifting across the room,
Fond thoughts evoke of a father, who sadly died too soon;
One of nature's gentlemen, he served in war and peace
His fellowman and countryside, with a love that never ceased.

From nature, music, books to travel . . . my girlhood all was filled
With ever growing awareness, that beyond the distant hills
Lay treasures of fauna and flora, just waiting to be found
Amid the buzz of bees in trees . . . in the music of countryside sounds.

Versed in ways from Viking days, and his wanderings thro' Norway
By bicycle . . . complete with camping kit, back-pack and primus . . .
in his way.
He revelled in his traveller's tales of fetes and fjords,
And I would sit astride a stool . . . his audience was never bored!

Uig, Ullapool and the Lairig Ghru . . . were all familiar names to him,
By beck and burn . . . on a mountain side, he'd rest his weary limbs;
And his love of desolation, he has bequeathed to me,
For off the well-worn track I go . . . in his steps that only I can see!

I suppose that as a child you take so much for granted,
You think that your parents are immortal . . . and you are always wanted;
Then one day you wake up, and find yourself an orphan . . .
The harsh reality that you're alone . . . how can you live without them?

But it's the quality . . . not the quantity of years that's important,
And you realise you wasted time by being self-indulgent;
For the value of a parent's wisdom, gained through years of learning,
Becomes apparent when your own child's attention's worth the earning!

Now silent tears course down my cheeks . . . but they are tears of joy,
A lasting memorial to one who gave me so much that'll never cloy.
So let the strains of Chopin . . . Tchaikovsky . . . and Liszt
Echo in my ears . . . to remind me of a friendship I'm so glad I never missed!

Jean Makin

YOU'RE STILL HERE FOR ME

Dad, your picture was taken.
It was sitting there with all my other things,
Inside my bag it was dad,
So I could look when I was sad.

I know you've gone dad,
I know you're in heaven,
But sometimes dad, when I was out,
I'd look at your picture and up at the clouds.

Why did they do it dad,
Why did they take my bag?
Everything in it, dad,
Including my glasses, dad.

You know what these mean to me,
You know I need them to see,
Why dad, I know what it's like to be blind,
And now I find it hard to see.

I searched for another pair, dad,
They are helping me to see,
All I want you to know dad,
You're still here for me.

Mary Jo West

MY MOODY AND CARING DAD

A laugh a minute dad
A cry a minute dad
A sombre dad
A wicked dad sometimes
But mostly dad.
Sometimes a hard, to stand dad
But always we agree, to disagree
My dad hopefully
Always my dad.

My dad my sweetest dad
We may not agree dad all the time
Sometimes life gets you down, depression hits you
But my dear dad you kick yourself out of it.
And are the same to me again -
I salute you dad -
For here and tomorrow.

Neville J Carson

LOVE EXCELLING

Did you really have to die and leave me dad,
In this world so full of grief and pain.
What can I do that is worthwhile
To find the will to live again.

We shared so much together.
We even thought and moved as one,
And in our special world of love,
Everyday, for us, the sun always shone.

But now I'm left here on my own
With time still left to live.
What can I do to make you proud of me?
What of my life is there left to give!

I'll find a way in time I know,
When the pain of loss begins to go.
I'll look at your photograph each new day,
And tell you all the things I've wanted to say.

For how I wish I had said those words,
I love you with all my heart.
But you knew, I'm sure, and not for long,
Will time be able to keep us apart.

Joan M Jones

MY DAD

Dad you gave me advice, that was always sound.
I wonder often, now you're not around.
I loved you dad, but you had to go
The weariness in you was beginning to show.
But your memory lingers, my love for you grows
Advice you gave with a goodness of heart
As only my dad could, straight from the heart.
A rough diamond were you, there are but a few,
Loved so deeply, as the dad I once knew
If I had a wish, I know what it would be
To have you dear dad, for a while here with me.

Joan Patrickson

PRIDE IN MY FATHER

So kind, caring, and full of love, oh my sweet dad,
you are mine, and I am yours, knowing you, I am so glad,
I cherish you, with all my loving heart and soul,
devotion and loyalty are parts of you, making you whole,
my dad works hard for all of us every single day,
helping out and protecting his family, all the way,
with all his six children, three sisters and brothers,
I adore my dad for everything he does for me and others,
he gives all his time and understanding to all of us,
with all his ill health and all his pain, without a fuss,
more than one in a million, my dad is one of a kind,
guardian of me and of my kin, you are decency defined,
all the things our dad does for us, we will all treasure,
father of mine, your warm heart is so big, beyond measure,
our dad, Donald Brian, is the best we could ever hope for,
always in our minds and thoughts, you are forever adored.

Josephine T Elliott

1992: A NICE YEAR FOR THE CUP

'I lost my way to Wembley' said Dad.
'I took the wrong tube and ended up at Brent Cross:
Thought I'd forgotten my ticket . . .
. . . What a day, 25th May . . . '

'Pardon?' I replied.
'I'm talking about the 1963 FA Cup Final.'
(Which City lost) 'Dad! We've never won!'
Dad's been saying 'Maybe this year . . . '
Ever since I remember!

Season 91/92 was special, though
City ended in the fourth round
After six years and a one-nil victory.
When extra time looked like 'Replay, here we come . . . '
Ace defender and 'favourite son'
Hammered the mighty sphere home.
'What's that?' asked Dad
'Kicked the ball! Scored the goal!' I replied
The whole stadium lit up
Twenty thousand faces smiling, January sun
I yelled and cheered for joy
Dad waved his scarf, spilled his coffee
Muttered something about 1963 . .
Suddenly impassioned I hugged him
Just as I did when I was a kid.
He put his woolly hat on my head and said:
'Nice year for the Cup, m'duck'.
Yes Dad. Nice year for the Cup.

Nick Brunel

DAD

My special dad,
Is the one who -
has waited beside me,
who comforted my spirit,
while holding my hand,
when I needed it most.
The dad who loved my smiles,
and was never afraid of my tears,
my only true friend,
who really cares about me,
my dad's cherished and loved,
more than he will ever know,
dad - you are my friend -
and a beautiful part of my life.

Lesley Baker

UNTITLED

Dad, I know at times we argue,
But it's not always that way,
Remember when I was young,
You would always come and play.

You always tried to teach me,
When I was going wrong,
And although I never listened,
You were right all along.

Dad, even though my life's been tough,
And I've taken many a wrong turn,
I do love you dad,
For all you've helped me learn.

Amanda Jervis

MY DAD

What can I say about my dad
He was small in stature, a 'bit of a lad'
He joined the Leicesters in WW1
Fought in the bloody battle on the Somme
With his father they fought side by side
My dad came home but his father died.

He lived and worked for his family
A jack of all trades one may say
For times were hard and money short
He was thankful for work that each day brought.
He was a brick maker, bricklayer, and chimney sweep
A stoker, and gardener as well
He taught me to dig, to plant and to hoe
I did very well for a 'gel'.
He taught me to ride a bike, fly a kite
Mend my own punctures as well.
Gave me away on my wedding day
What stories of him I can tell.
When WW2 came he joined the Home Guard
Still wanting to do his bit, proud of the uniform he wore
With gas mask and fire lighting kit
I respected my dad and though he was strict
I now realise why he was so.
My two brothers and I he kept in check
And when he said no, he meant no.

When I looked at his medals from WW1
A Military Medal I see
Given for bravery on the field
My dad was a hero to me.

Kathleen McQueen

FATHER OF MINE

Father you are the world to me
although I don't always show it
But deep down in the heart of me
I think you really know it.
The names I called you when I was young
I didn't mean a word,
The words I write you in this poem
Will show how much I care.
I love you dad, I always will
No matter where or when
and hope these words will last forever
I've written them in pen.
The pen may fade as time goes by
Of that there is no doubt.
One thing is for sure -
These words can't be rubbed out.
In my heart forever
Love you every day
I wish I could have said these words
Before you went away. God bless. I love you.

Julie Jones

MY DAD

Daddy oh daddy I know you're the best
When I went around the world and I saw all the rest
They haven't the humour the wit or the charm
And I feel very proud to have you on my arm.

Whenever I suffered a time of despair
I looked for your shoulders, I knew they'd be there
No millions of miles can keep us apart
For wherever I go you are there in my heart.

There isn't a time, I can say that's gone by
When the sparkle has left those electric blue eyes
Your smile is warm and puts me at ease
Your laughter is comfort and reassures me.

I look back on the wonderful years that I've had
With a mother that dotes and a hard working dad
I'll never forget all the things that you do
And I'll never stop saying how much I love you.

Gillian Conners

DEAR OLD DAD

Dad did say, 'You think life's a game'.
I did it my way, just the same.
Dad was so sweet and kind,
but nonetheless, the sort, you mind.
He could look very stern, you see,
and so I took him seriously.
Sometimes he'd burst into song and dance,
brought on with joy, but by chance.
He was always so serene,
and brave and stoic in between.
He was also very reliable,
and that's not deniable,
when he got to his house gate,
he was never, at home late,
you could set the clock,
by his footsteps and door knock.
A great legacy, he gave to me,
to take life calmly, as did he.
My dependable dear old dad,
when he died, I was so sad.

Doreen Frost

MY DAD

So special was my dad,
Cheeky, naughty as a lad.
But honest as the day was long,
Kind, gentle and handsome.
No, he wasn't really Clark Gable
Yet, he was so able.
To pick me up and sweetly say
'You're my girl' I'd hear him say.
Yes, I was his girl
His loving child
Yes I was like him, naughty and wild.
But in a quiet loving way
I still talk to him in my own way.
He listens too,
I know he does
Just like he used to do,
To all my troubles and my woe,
And yet he kindly answers me,
And in his own dear gentle voice
'I'm still with you, my daughter'.
And I shut my eyes and think,
I wish you were 'my dad'.

Florence Brice

FATHER

F or all the things you share.
A lways there showing you care.
T o me you'll always be my dad.
H elping me when I feel sad.
E very little thing you do.
R eminds me of why I love you.

Barbara Eyre

104

WELCOME HOME DAD

I remember, I remember,
The photo on the wall,
Of a soldier, young and handsome,
Standing proud, and tall,

I remember, I remember,
The day he went away,
To fight for king and country,
To be gone, for many a day.

I remember, I remember,
The tears, and the pain,
The watching, and the waiting,
For him to come back home again.

I remember, I remember,
Four long years, without a dad,
Wanting him safe at home,
No more feeling sad.
I remember, I remember,
The day he walked back through the door,
He didn't look, quite the same,
As he did before,
          Not like the soldier, in the photo on the wall.
His face was lined and weary,
His eyes, they looked so sad,
But to me, a little child,
He was still my lovely *dad*,
So I put my arms around him,
And climbed upon his knee,
And I welcomed back, this soldier *dad*,
Who meant all the world to me.

Jacqueline C Davies

MY DAD

Dad was kind and full of fun,
He loved us lots, both me and mum.
If I felt low, or sad inside,
I knew in dad I could confide.
He'd tell me stories about the war -
And days long past when folk were poor.
He enjoyed making children's toys
For friends' and neighbours' girls and boys.
Wooden forts for little soldiers, and wooden carts with painted bricks,
A little farm with cows and horses, and woolly sheep and baby chicks!
Christmas morn, was fun to see,
We'd both hung stockings by the tree;
I got toys and coloured chalks,
Dad got coal, and cabbage stalks!
We'd go for walks, play on the swings
And laugh and talk of childish things.
The years passed by and we grew older,
Now dad could lean upon *my* shoulder.
But now he's making angels laugh with crazy jokes and silly pranks -
For all your love and comfort dad, my heartfelt, true, and grateful *thanks!*

May Robin

CLAN

My dad is in the garden,
Watering some plants,
I ask him if he needs help,
And he replies 'no thanks',
Later I bring him a cup of tea,
As he takes the mug he smiles at me.

We watch a video together,
Nearly every night,
Dad always gets thrillers,
He knows what I like,
Even when they make me scared,
My dad will always be my friend.

He takes us on holiday to Scotland,
It is where he was born,
We go to a pretty loch,
And stay there all day long,
Dusk, hears goodbyes, from a man and his daughter,
But they leave their warm imprint on the water.

Carly Vickers

MY FATHER

It's so sad
        Being on your own
It's so sad
        Sitting in your room all alone
The pain and the suffering
        that you are going through
I want you to know
        how much I love you
I feel your pain inside my heart
        wishing I only could be with you
Instead of being so many miles apart
        is why I'm feeling blue
We have had some good times
        and we have had some bad
But most of all
        you are my dad.

Anthony Clarke

THE FRENCH VISIT

I look down onto the grave of the young
        soldier that died
It's very hard to describe without tears
        flowing down onto this page
At 29 he seems such a baby now to my sixty
        years in age
My feelings are laid bare as I remember his
        bright smile and dark curly hair
a humour that did a Chaplin take-off with
        feet turned out and stick twirling aloft
He would hug my mum and rub his prickly chin
        on my face making me shriek
but his hands would be gentle as he stroked
        my baby sister's cheek
I watched as the soldier went marching off to
        war
but telling my aunt he would not come back of
        that he was sure
his intuition proved him quite right he died
        fighting the great fight
A grave in France was his reward and even now
        I wrestle with anger at our Lord
and maybe it all seems such a long time ago
        but he was my *dad* and I loved him so.

Barbara Wheeler

WALKED AWAY

You looked so peaceful laying there
No sorrows, worries, or worldly care
I begged, please don't do this to me
You could not hear, you could not see

I tried to raise you
From your sleep
I could not do it
It was too deep.

So I kissed you on the cheek
Through my tears I could not speak
I could not find the words to say
So I turned and walked away.

Dave Hesmer

GOOD MEMORIES OF DAD

My dad the strong and silent type,
tall, good looking too.
A forester on large estate,
hard work, his job to do.

Born in bonny Banffshire,
into farming stock.
Champion of the underdog,
his brain, and eyes, like hawk.

He always gave us good advice,
his talents too were many.
He told us if we had good health,
we didn't need a penny.

If ever help was needed
my dad would answer call.
A hero in our childish eyes
to us, he did walk tall.

He lived till he was 95,
accepted life's demand.
He's gone, but not forgotten
his memory still commands.

C Shanks

MY DAD

He came out of nowhere,
And rescued my life,
He took all my worries,
Made my mother his wife,
I wasn't his child,
When I was first born,
But I know that the bond,
Can never be torn,
Without him our lives,
Would be much different now,
For he brought me up,
And he taught me how,
Every Christmas, every birthday,
Of my life was the best,
For he made it happen,
He would never rest,
Now I am much older,
His job with me is done,
If I can choose a dad in my next life,
He's sure to be the one.

Michelle Chrystie

MY PAL DAD

My pal dad is a wonderful guy
He's firm but funny,
Strict and brave
And always there when I need him.

My pal dad plays football with me
And sometimes takes me go-karting.
He's great fun
To be with
And I couldn't be without him.

Mark Buckley (10)

DAD YOU WERE SPECIAL

Dad you were special
I thought the world of you.
Then you got ill and had to leave
And you broke my heart in two.
You radiated happiness
You were everyone's best friend.
You sorted out their problems
They gave you things to mend.
Neighbours' children called you granddad
And often came to stay.
They always had one of your sweets
Before going on their way.
My childhood memories are happy ones
Locked in my heart forever.
And your lovely smile and kind ways
Will stay with me to the end of my days.

Irene Corin

FOREVER IN MY HEART

I still feel the pain
Like a constant pouring rain
I felt so helpless and sad
When I lost you dear dad
I can't forget that cold dark day
The memory never fades away
There's not a day goes by
I don't think of you and sigh
I miss you so much
Your warm gentle touch
Even though you're long gone
Precious memories linger on
I know we'll never part
You're forever in my heart.

Nicholas Fletcher

DAD

I miss you so, why did you have to go?
Was it something I said, I need to know

Can I be forgiven for driving away?
What will I do again what will I say?

If a bridge could be built I would build it
Every second every single minute!

If I thought we could be together again
In peace and harmony, without the strain!

Turn the tables I would be different too
I would love and be so proud of you

Instead of pushing you out and away
Okay you win I'll go to Gateway!

Debra Neale

MY DAD - MY HERO (1923-1993)

Wherever I am, whatever I do
My thoughts keep coming back to you.
A man so big - a man so strong,
You taught me what was right and wrong.
You gave me laughter, you gave me hope
You always had the strength to cope.
You told me tales about the war
Oh how I wish you could once more.
I miss you in each passing day
and in this poem, I'd like to say . . .
I live in hope that I can be
as special to mine as you were to me.

Wendy Forbes

TO DAD AFTER MY WEDDING DAY

I well remember the day I was wed,
It was gone 8 o'clock when I jumped out of bed.
Nervously, mother walked into the room
Carrying her duster and clutching a broom.

'Well, I don't suppose there's anything
you want to know?'
She asked, and her face turned pink.
'You've probably learnt it all
from those office girls!'
And I gave her a knowing wink.

> We arrived at the church,
> The car gave a lurch
> And we almost tumbled out.
> I talked to my bridesmaid
> outside the church door,
> And dad hissed
> 'Please, don't shout!'

After the ceremony the cameras clicked
And several aunties cried
and made their eyes red.

Dad's friend took my bridegroom aside
and said:

'I've got some advice for you,
young lad

You will always take second place
to her dad!'

Marion Hacker

CHRISTMAS WILL COME AGAIN
(dedicated to my late father - Gordon Smith who died 8th March 1989 -
loved and remembered always)

Oh dad do you remember the days,
Of tickled ribs and snowball fights,
Father and daughter hand in hand,
Both bemused by the Christmas lights.

Then my tiny fingers gripped round yours,
As we paddled at the edge of the sea,
And my first day at school,
When apparently you shed more tears than me.

You were a proud man,
And it wasn't all picnics and perfection,
But I always knew beneath that tough exterior,
Lay a world of deep love and affection.

At times your passing feels like yesterday,
Then suddenly it's been longer than forever,
But the love between a father and daughter,
Is something even death cannot sever.

I sense you all around me guiding, protecting,
So near I can almost touch,
I hope you sense me too dad,
And know you're missed so very much.

My world is here for now,
It is not my time yet,
But I will love you always,
I will never forget.

Rest in peace my darling dad,
Sleep easy - some day I will wake you and then,
We will walk hand in hand, smiling,
To see the Christmas lights together once again.

Anna Maria Carr

A DAD

A dad is a man
Such a good clever man
And there's no-one can do
What a clever dad can

A plumber, a painter
A jack of all trade
All of his gifts
Must be heavenly made

A bike with a puncture
He'll cleverly mend
If you're short of a tenner
He'll eagerly lend

If it's raining outside
He'll give you his car
He's a good, kind man
Too generous by far

He's there to protect you
And make you feel glad
That your happy, healthy
And not feeling sad

A kiss on your forehead
To bring on a smile
And if anyone hurt you
He'd chase them a mile

This is why dad is a man
Such a good, clever man
And there's no-one can do
What a clever dad can!

Mandy Meredith

SUPERDAD

Sleeping in the armchair,
Gardening in his vest
Shouting at the telly,
These are things
That dad does best.
Looking for his car keys
Stepping on the cat,
Telling mum to hush
Because now England's in to bat.
Tutting at the shopping bill,
Locking up the phone,
Telling six foot hippies
That his daughter's not at home.
These are the things
That make our dad
The same as all the rest
Except that our dad
Is the one
That we all love the best.

J Gibson

MY FAETHER

A man of many words my faether,
Not many would reach a preacher's favour.
But he means little by way of malice,
Perhaps a dictionary should be his practice.
As children we were rarely clouted,
But hell we ran when faether shouted.

So as I make my way through life,
And I have found my chosen wife,
I can see through clearer eyes
The man behind the noise and size,
And a better man I'll never meet,
My faether.

Ian Kennedy

A DAUGHTER'S LOVE

The ground was so hard sitting there inside the subway gate,
My knees pulled up inside my dress, there I'd patiently wait.
My back it felt so cold then, leaning against the tiled wall,
The echo of silence, my ears aching, as I listen for its call,
Suddenly I would hear it! That distant rumbling sound,
Getting closer, ever closer, my heart would start to pound.
Its horn blows! Its brakes screech! It pulls into the station,
I hear voices and footsteps, each with the same motivation.
Like a stampede they go by me, as if I wasn't there,
I search the giants' faces, I can't see him anywhere.
There! He's coming towards me, my tiny heart skips a beat,
The man I love has seen me, it's him I've come to meet.
He lift me up and cuddles me, then takes my tiny hand,
As dad and I walk home to tea, aren't memories grand!
Alas! He's long since gone from me, but those days I still recall,
For a daughter's love for her dad is the greatest love of all.

M S Kennedy

WHAT IS A FATHER?

A father is someone who scolds you when you come in late,
Who ticks you off for looking such a state,
A father is someone who rubs your tummy when you are sick,
And who gives you his football numbers to pick,
A father is someone who wades into the river to save you from the tide,
Who picks you up and gives you a piggy-back ride,
A father is someone who gives you extra pocket money, 'Ssh, don't tell
                                                    your mother',
Who's grumpy at times but you wouldn't choose another,
A father to me is many things,
But most of all he is
Love, cuddles, tears and joy,
Many years separate the man from the boy
And although he is gone his memory lives on
God bless my father.

Diane Chisholm

GRAVES AND LARKIN

My father had no regard for poets.
So when two died within a week,
he curled his lip at all the media attention.
Annoyed him, so to speak.
Now, of course, if it had been the case of a jockey
or a footballer,
I'd have been treated to all the old stories from his youth.
Preferred sport to words, my father;
a touch uncouth.
And yet, I suppose in my few final hours,
when all is deathly dry and dim,
a poet's words will fail to move me.
Just as in life they didn't him.

Malcolm Brown

118

DON'T CRY LENA

As a child I had a mother my father
Packed,. upped and left,
I knew his face I had pictures
I fought and his name I kept.

No birthday cards did I receive
No Christmas presents - large or small,
In my mind I used to wonder
If he cared for me at all.

How can a child understand the things that
Grown-ups say and do,
My aunt's words to this day still haunt me
'Your daddy never wanted you'.

I'd scream, cry and pull her hair
I don't believe you tell the truth,
Grandad would take me in his arms
'Don't cry Lena - I love you'.

Grandad was to me my father he provided
Security in the home
He gave me anything I wanted
He taught me everything I know,
Never did I have reason to fear him
He loved and raised me as his own.

Selena Pearce

TO DAD

Today I picked a rose for you.
Today I cried a tear for you.
Today I smile as I remember you.
Today I thank you just for being you!
Thanks for all the good times.
Sorry for the bad.
Shared so many memories.
Happy ones and sad.
Years full of laughter.
Years full of tears.
A treasury of memories.
Raining down the years.
Fishing rods and railway trains,
Building bricks and football games,
Picture books and teddy bears.
Thanks for showing that you cared.
When we needed someone strong.
You were there to lean upon.
Shared our worries.
Bore our pain.
Gave us knowledge.
Took the strain.
Today I picked a rose for you.
Today I cried a tear for you.
Today I smile as I remember you.
Today I thank you just for being you.

Janice L Williams

DEAR DAD

I've been saving up my pennies
To buy a special treat
It's not something that you wear
Or something that you eat

It is something for my father
That I'll give him Father's Day
A verse set in a silver frame
With this I want to say

Thank you for the love you give
When I'm feeling down
You know it's such a comfort
In having you around

I know sometimes I'm naughty
In fact be downright bad
But that's why children growing up
Need a patient dad

Your love shows in the things you do
You worry and you care
You guide me and protect me
When I fall you're always there

When I'm grown up, and am a man
With a wife and children too
I hope my children love me
Like I, dear dad, love you.

Don Woods

DAD

He had a lovely smile so I was told
this soldier who could not die old
he was killed in the year of '44
my dad who fought in the second world war
a man I know only by a photograph
am told he liked a really good laugh
tallish, slim build with brown wavy hair
always playing jokes and loved a challenging dare
5 medals are all I own of my brave young dad
he was full of fun and a bit of a lad
in his uniform he was a handsome sight
when he laid down his life one February night
I never remember my dad, but he saw me
just a tiny baby on his knee
I often wonder how my life would be
if there had just been dad, mum and me
How can you miss someone you do not know
but you can feel the love of the family as you grow
the older I got I knew he loved me
am so sad that what went before just had to be.

Janet Snowsill

MY DEAR OLD DAD

When I was a little girl
To me you were a giant
Laughing, encouraging, patient
(Even when I was defiant)
And I adored you.

When I was a teenager
We put the world to right
Had such heated arguments
(Always a verbal fight)
And I thought I knew more than you.

The day that I got married
You rushed me down the aisle
Gave me away with confidence
(Wearing a great big smile)
But I knew you'd miss me.

Now you're in your eighties
Our relationship isn't bad
I've learned wisdom through the years
You're now
My dead old dad.

Greta Thomas

MY HERO

He was just an ordinary man,
I will describe him if I can,
Because no words will be enough
For such a gentle but tough guy.
His humour, his constant smile
Would always beguile most folk.
He knew hard times
And worried much,
But even then was ready with a joke,
And would clutch each chance
To rise above his fate.
I feel so glad that I told him
Of my love
Before it was too late.
One of nature's 'gents',
My dad I can't replace.
His smiling face is with me now
In memory and I vow
Will always be
The dearest man in all the world to me.

Freda Tester-Ellis

DEAR DAD

I wish I knew my father
I wouldn't tell him lies
I'd let him know that it's okay
Whatever his alibis.

The wind that rings the changes
Has sung a song for me
I ain't ungrateful to you, Sam
Just the mixed-up part you see.

I wouldn't expect open arms
From wherever my father is
Just that he be proud of me
For doing things like this.

But I know that mum and Sam are glad
That I made it on my own
Yet I wonder if anyone sees the tears
Of this sad but gifted clown.

Unhappy little girl in me
Call quiet for your dad
He may not be your flesh and blood
But he's the best you could have had.

Julie Ashpool

FISHING WITH DAD

I went with my dad, to fish in the lake
Sat on the bank and threw the fish cake,
He sent me for gentles to bait up his hooks
'And while you're about it, bring my Wellington boots!'

I looked at him, and I gave a great sigh
What is the matter?' he shouted at me!
'Oh nothing' said I, with a glint in my eye!
But oh how I wished, I'd been a great Russian spy!

I went down to the river to fish with my dad
And how I remember it wasn't too bad,
I'm sure he said he wished I'd been a lad
I didn't mind fishing with line and a hook

But I didn't like handling, that slimy wee fluke,
I've been fishing again, on that same river bank
But it isn't the same without my dear old dad.

Elizabeth Kelly

UNTITLED
*(In tribute to my wonderful father who suddenly
passed away just before Father's Day after many years apart)*

Dearest daddy, be now at rest,
You gave your all, you gave your best.
From my heart I love you so,
Still be there for me, where're you go.

You rest near God's creatures in 'Squirrels Glade',
'Neath sunshine and flowers, and cooling shade.
Be at peace in heaven where you deserve to be,
Give a sign and call and I will hasten to thee.

Thank you for loving me and being my dad,
I will try hard to be cheerful and not too sad.
Be now united with your own loving mum
Who has waited so long for you, her own dear son.

From Vicky, dear daddy, you are locked in my heart,
So soon again we are forced to part.
When the time is right I will share in your glade,
Life's memories, and moments, that will never fade.

Rest now dear daddy with the squirrels close by,
Beneath the trees, amid the flowers, and under God's sky.

Vicky Mills

MY DEAR OLD DAD

My dad's a window cleaner,
A master at his trade
There isn't a better cleaner,
That's where his fortune's made.
Up the ladder he would climb
With wiper, bucket and sponge,
He'd wipe away all the grime
Until the job was done.
Oh, how my dad enjoyed his task,
How happy he did seem,
He made light work of all the graft
To get those windows clean.
I'm proud of my dear old dad
There isn't anyone finer
And after a thought I think I'm glad
That I should be his minor.
And when he'd done his daily task
And homeward bound he'll be,
The only thing that I will ask
That he will sit with me.
I'd gaze upon his weary face
As he sips his cup of tea
And as he stares into space,
Is he thinking of me?
Perhaps one day when I am grown
He'll find a place for me,
In the firm he calls his own,
His cleaning company.
And as his firm does prosper,
I would hear him say
'All this did I foster
In my independent way!'

Thomas Pritchard

TO MY DAD

Only you deserve
A rhyme like this
Because of all your trouble
I'm sending you a kiss

I know I've never said
Not really anyway
But, I love you dad
That's all I have to say.

You have always been there
With help and advice
You've always been straight
To me that's nice

At one time we feared
As it was touch and go
It made me sit and think
How much I love you so.

I couldn't understand why
You were - oh so bad
When I saw how ill you were
It made me very sad.

But now you've pulled through
And I would just like to say
That I really do love you
And it grows day by day.

You are a lovely smashing chap
I just wish the whole world knew
This is a special rhyme
Just from me, sent to you.

Theresa Regan

MY FATHER

Father was a big, strong man
When I was small to him I ran,
Knowing he would keep from harm
Shelter me within his arm.

Father was so gentle when
I was hurt and in some pain.
Kind and caring, loving too,
He'd do anything for you.

Father Christmas never missed
(My father checked he had my list).
Easter eggs each year appeared,
That they would not I never feared.

Father made me a doll's house
It kept me quiet as a mouse.
Playing with this lovely toy
Then became my fav'rite ploy.

Now I'm old I think of him,
The mem'ries never will grow dim
Of one who meant so much to me
That in my heart he'll ever be.

Joyce M Turner

THE SOLDIER

The war was over the battle won.
You were coming home, your fighting done.
My face was scrubbed, my hair was curled.
You had never seen your little girl.
The middle of night, a knock on the door,
I was woken gently, my eyes were all sore.
I looked at the man who had tears in his eyes,
'Hello daddy', then everyone cried.

B Liles

PROUD SONS!

Three little boys were talking
of the jobs their fathers had.
'My dad works in an office'
said the first proud little lad.

'He fills out forms and papers.
It's a good job he has got.
I'm not sure what he's earning
but I know he's paid a lot.'

The second boy was not put off
and he couldn't wait to say
'I think my father earns the most.
He's famous anyway'.

'My father is an artist
and his pictures always sell.
We've got a really big house
and a sailing boat as well.'

'That's nothing' said the third boy,
'for my dad's a vicar, see.
He talks for just a little while
and then collects a fee.'

'They pass some bags around the church.
Do you know' said the lad
'it takes four men to carry up
the money for my dad!'

John Christopher Cole

FATHER'S DAY

My father is all I want to be
He's humorous wise and kind
And loved by all that know him
His equal hard to find

He even makes my mother smile
At the end of a trying day
And with his words of wisdom
He banishes my fears away

Whenever he works away from home
Directly he has gone
Everything's in a turmoil
Everything seems to go wrong

When dad returns he soon sorts out
With patience and with skill
The problems that await him
His duties to fulfil

My father is my hero
And I know that in the end
When I grow up we'll always be
The very best of friends

Isabel Poilly

A FATHER'S FAREWELL

She glowed with love, my daughter -
(this double of my wife)
White robed, and beautiful to see - and
going from my life.
I held her close and kissed her - and
words were hard to say . . .
I loved her more than ever - on
this, her wedding day.

She shone with joy, my daughter - this
part of me so dear -
How can I bear the emptiness when
she has gone from here?
My wife came close and whispered
'My dear one, don't be sad
Another joy she's brought to us - the
son we never had'

I proudly led my daughter, towards
her chosen man -
My heart was overflowing - as only
a father's can . . .
She whispered, oh, so softly - I
had to strain to hear;
'I love him, 'cos he's like
you dad'
And thus - dispelled my fear..

Dorothy Whiteley

MY DAD

My dad he means the world to me,
For I love him and he loves me.
He's always there to talk to,
And help when things go bad.
Someone to tell secrets to,
And help when I am sad.
When I was just a little girl,
There was always time to play.
I would wait for him to come back home,
The same time every day.
But now I am getting older,
And learn to do things on my own.
I know I've dad to lean on,
And the love that's there at home.

Marie L Wainwright (12)

MY DAD

My dad was a wonderful man,
In the war he drove a tank.
Most of his friends died
But he survived,
Everyone said he had nine lives.

When I was three I used to sit on his knee,
He tickled me till I cried,
My friends all used to envy me,
He was so full of fun and frivolity.

When I was twenty-one,
He gave me away to the man I loved.
What a day we all had,
My relatives all arrived and said how great I looked,
But I shed a tear to be leaving my dad.

When he died oh how I cried,
for the man who had been my best friend
All of my life,
I miss him every day that dawns
The man that made me the way that I am.

Your dad can never be replaced,
So make haste to tell him how you feel,
When he's gone life is never the same
A door is shut to remain locked inside your heart,
Your feelings of love that cannot be explained.

Jacqueline Bentley

MY DAD
(Dedicated to Ernest Clarke CPO L10304 RN)

My dad he was a naval man in two world wars served he
for twenty-eight years the seven seas he did sail,
A proud man who served in ships of grey in the Royal Navy
and the medals on his chest are proof his loyalty did not fail.

When serving in the Arctic seas they told him his son is born
another two years to pass before homeward he could be,
A love for me and his duty to the crown he would be torn
until the day to his family and his son to hold and see.

Then off to the Far East and to China he had to go
another few years away missing my mum and me,
He went up the Yellow River to fight the foe
who is this man my father my mum said I will see.

Then home he came to bring lots of gifts for his wife and son
silk kimonos (I have one still) and funny Chinese toys,
These are still in the family - of China a memory gone
then telegram return to ship, message that annoys.

Around the world he sailed once more
writing letters to mum and me,
Is this a sailor's duty chore?
When will my dad come home for us to see.

When the time came for him to sail no more
so glad was my mum to know he was homeward bound,
Then came that conflict the Second World War
from mum's bedroom I heard a sobbing sound.

I never had the joy of having a dad
at home each night and weekend,
A life without a father can be sad
but proud of him I am, that man to sea they would send.

John Clarke

POEM FOR DAD

Dad was loved throughout his life
By his children and his dear wife
He was the family's heart and soul
He had rules we had to obey
But was right at end of day.
We had no car and no TV,
But had holidays by the sea.
Dad joined in the games we played
Read us stories at end of day.
All of us loved our dear dad
Although at times we were bad.
He worked hard in his trade
A senior position he had made
Well respected in high esteem
Managed well his working team.
He helped others all over town
His goodwill was well known.
Dad taught us right from wrong
To be polite and morals strong.
Loved too our dear mum - his wife
They shared good times in his life.
He was the best - our dad,
And looking back - I'm glad.

Sheila Waller

DEAR DAD

I was just thirteen when mama passed away,
And even after all these years, it seems like yesterday,
I was so afraid, but you took me in your arms and held me tight,
As I listened to your voice I knew that you,
Would make everything turn out all right.

You showed your love and tenderness in so many ways,
I realise now that for you they were very difficult days,
As I grew up when I did wrong you were always strict but fair,
And the most important thing to me, was you were always there,
To comfort me when things went wrong,
I felt safe knowing that your love for me was strong.

I never got to tell you,
How much you meant to me,
And the things that I remember most was your smile,
How you used to sit me on your knee,
And you would tell me that I was special,
These happy memories will always remain with me,
And even though we are now far apart,
Dad you will always have a special place deep within my heart.

Terri Brant

IN MY FATHER'S TIME

He saw the airships glow over Glasgow
The first planes whine with asthma.

He saw the hungry years before Hitler
Rose his hand over Europe's peace.

He saw action in Germany, crossed the Rhine
Came back to the sackcloth and ashes of Auschwitz.

He heard the crack of the atom
The bomb that came soft as a kiss on Hiroshima.

He saw a man on the moon
And the globe roll round to war, big as the bang
That built the beautiful world.

Now he stands at the window, watching
Wondering if he and the end will meet.

Kenneth C Steven

MY DAD

My old man's a scrapman
he works hard day and night,
and when he comes home mucky
he really is a sight.
No matter what the weather
he works on the tip,
no wonder he gets flu
and his back does give him gip.
He has to strip the cable
and then he goes and burns,
he tries to finish quickly
'cos for the pub he yearns.
His car is a shed
his pick-up is the pits,
they are always breaking down
and falling all to bits.
I wish I could win the lottery
so my dad he could retire,
then I'd go down to his work
and set the lot on fire.

Dawn Scanlon

MY OLD MAN

My old man's a funny old man
Of that you must agree;
He's got no hair on the top of his head
In the place where his hair ought to be.

He likes naught better than to visit a pub;
If you take him he'll be willing
To strum the piano and sing along
All night for just a shilling!

And when it's time to close the doors
He'll need your helping hand
To guide him back towards his home
'Cause he finds it hard to stand.

But all the same there are none like him,
He's unique of his kind;
He's content to watch the world go by
And never seems to mind.

Geoff Tullett

MY FATHER IN HEAVEN

Dear father, I was young when you left,
Not a rep, selling macs, but a rep
Of this earth and you left me bereft,
Taking one irrevocable step.
Your devotion to God I recall;
Is your talisman yet Book of Psalms?
Does traditional holy prayer shawl
Still deck with silk reverential arms?
Your power, your strength, these must persist
And the laughter that about you spread,
Your devotion to the wife you kissed -
My mamma - can it be true *she's* dead?
If your ghost knows me does it perceive
I wilt at music's note - almost die?
And, swamped by its wonderment, still grieve
About life's impermanence and cry?
Bruch's 'Kol Nidrei' falls about my ears
And father, dear, I hear you praying
When your loving too pervades my tears,
Your blessing deep in Maestro's playing.

Ruth Daviat

BETTER LATE THAN NEVER

I stare at the clock, he's late again!
Why am I surprised? It's always the same,
I'm only his daughter, after all
And I etched in his mind, the time to call
So as I stand and wait, the rain begins
My feet turn numb from the puddles they're in,
My spirits dampened, I soulfully sigh
and stamp my feet in anger and wonder why!
He's always late and never seems to care
how long he keeps me waiting there.
A birthday party, he doesn't arrive!
I fight to keep the anger locked inside.
Invited to a meal, I spend so much time
he's late, he smiles, he doesn't mind.
I cry for the thoughts that are so bad
when I think of the countless let-downs I've had
and all the times I've waited in the rain
knowing he's going to be late again.
But his heart is kind, his generosity overawes
and it's on the best points I must focus most of all.
Because if lateness is his only sin
and it's heavenly goodness he's bathed in
I'll be patient and keep my anger at bay
knowing he'll be late forever one day.

Kathryn L Cowling

DAD

Dads are only human
Ours is human too
He's outwith description
Except for simply blue
Groomed above his lip now
As he's always been
Carefully closely cropping
Hair from dark to new

138

Yorkshire's thanks by distance
Even when he's close
Gives our father's presence
Strength so thankfully most
And as thoughtful moments
Reach a reader's glare
He's at least a reason
Rhymes like this are fair

Thanks dear dad for hosting
Bennetts one to three
And for caring quietly
Even through our tree
That with hanging branches
Across a sea so wide
Through years' opened doorway
Written on both sides

David A Bennett

WHAT MAKES A DAD

What really makes a real father,
is it someone who's always nagging you about
your school work and makes you try harder.
Is it someone who's married to your biological mum,
or someone who's always at the pub filling up his tum.
Is it someone who really loves and cares for you,
or someone that really doesn't have a clue.
All these qualities you have to put in mind,
there's the good things and the bad things
that you have to put behind.
My dad cares for me, mum, my sister and even the cat too,
he always puts us first, I never know what to do.
My dad's excellent he beats all the rest,
he loves us and we love him, that's why he's the best.

K L Hayley (14)

FATHER'S DAY

Father's Day is just as important
in a way,
As that extra special moment
which comes on Mother's Day,
Fathers play their role in life
The breadwinner it seems,
To our dearest mother he's the
man of her dreams,
We shower him with gifts galore,
woolly socks, sent by the score -
But the main thing we portray
for Father's Day,
Is our perfect love no more -
He is a status symbol our
father dear,
We love to pamper him
Now Father's Day is here,
Breakfast in bed brought
on a tray,
With his favourite aftershave
for wash and brush up
for the day,
It always remains special
Father's Day for us each year,
A time of joy and merriment,
Just like Christmas cheer.

Denise Frost

A BAG OF PENNIES

In terms of time in my life
It's quite a long time ago
The seasons changed with the wildlife
As I'd play with my toy flamingo

Bursting with excitement
Sis and I (with mum and dad) were in a feverish daze
We'd skip along the pavement
'Twas our special day at Walton-on-the-Naze

Sandcastles made upon the beach
Fun-fair rides and candyfloss
Oh - nothing seemed out of reach
And mum and dad were never cross

But I wouldn't eat a hot dog
Thinking it was someone's pet
Misunderstanding this dialogue
I really was upset

Later dad would scurry away
Arriving at the pier penny slot machines
So definitely well-off
As he gave us a bag of pennies

Years later I did visit
These haunts of yesteryear
Returning is never so exquisite
But for these memories, I shed a tear

Peggy Ruth Banks

THE COBBLER

In case our shoes needed repair
Dad always kept an eye
If ever it poured, down with rain
Our feet remained quite dry

Our dad would go to the shops
Just before the wintry weather
Under his arm, when he came out
Was a very large piece of leather

With hammer, tacks and cobbler's foot
He's work into the night
And if it got too dark to see
He'd work, by candlelight

From the shed came the noise
As the hammer drove home the tacks
And after the leather cut and filed
Sealed, with cobbler's wax

At work his hours were very long
At home he did not rest
As he sat cobbling shoes
So we could look, our best

Dennis N Davies

THE HEART THAT CRIES

I too have cried on Breedon Hill,
As did my father, I lie quiet and still,
He was weeping for his tiny child,
I saw in his tears a child had smiled.

To become an angel, worldly life so brief,
Leaves behind a father's grief,
But gentle be the man that cries,
Heaven in his heart where my love lies.

My heart cried too as father talked,
I, tiny child this earth never walked,
But this sinful world will never afflict,
I a child, Jesus has picked.

How true the love in his soul that cried,
In my father's heart I will ever reside,
There to rest, its love adore,
There be my heaven for evermore.

Jack Hodges

A WISH

I wish I'd kissed my dad, some fifty years ago.
Such a quiet gentleman, a happy one to know
I wish I could have had a hug
Or perhaps a little fuss
Kissing is for girls he said
Not for men like us.
No doubt he thought a lot of me
But only shook my hand
Mam was different, she would kiss
When I was ill or hurt.
She would kiss me better
When dad was not alert
Dad would kiss his cornet, for he was in a band
His rendering of a solo part was really from the heart
'I dreamt I dwelt in marble halls'
Filled me with such emotions,
I never knew I had.
Now all the years have gone
I wish I'd kissed my dad.

Frederick Dyer

MY DAD

I got my character from my dad
And I think it's true to tell
According to other people
I got my looks as well
never once did he moan
As his hair was wrenched out
By a brush or a comb
He never looked at it as being a chore
As hour after hour, he sat cross legged
on the floor
Repairing dolls with dismembered limbs
Trying to reconcile my whims
He played the harmonica with such style
And I would sing all the while
Hardly the classics at this stage
More like the popular tunes of the age
'Me and my Shadow' we used to do
'On Mother Kelly's Doorstep' too
So very handsome, you had to say that
In his gabardine raincoat and trilby hat
So debonair with wit and charm
I was proud to walk out on his arm
He is always there for me, no matter what
And I know my lifestyle has worried him
a lot
But he has never had to fear
Because I am always very near
My love and affection he has won
'Cos he's the only man that I can count
on, *my dad* . . .

Anne Sherwood

BILLY BELL MM

My father was a soldier,
He was almost seventeen.
He wasn't really old enough,
He should have been eighteen.

The sergeant said 'How old are you?'
My dad said 'Seventeen'
'Well, go around the block son,
And come back when you're eighteen'.

My father did as the sergeant bid,
Came back a year older!
In less time than it takes to tell,
My father was a soldier!

He went to France, was decorated
Where the poppies grow,
Even though he really
Wasn't old enough to go.

Two years passed, a telegram
Came to my mother's door.
'Missing' it said,
'Presumed dead'
The sergeant gave a roar.

The sergeant was my father,
He had a twinkle in his eye.
'It's a good job I was home on leave,
Dead men tell no lies!'

My father was a soldier
He was almost seventeen,
He wasn't really old enough,
He should have been eighteen.

Doreen McKenzie

A BIT LATE, BUT THANKS DAD

I know that your shingles have made you feel low
But here are some things I thought you should know.

When boys are small, they all try to be
Just like their dad, it's so plain to see.

'Cause dads are our model, a guide to us all
Always reliable, always so tall.

Whenever we need them, whatever our plight
Dad's always there to make it all right.

My bike's got a puncture dad, can you please fix it?
Please take me fishing dad, can I have a biscuit?

I'll be ever so good dad, I'll always behave
I'm nearly a big boy dad, teach me to shave.

To be like their dad, most young men do strive
Dad, do you think you could teach me to drive?

I'm off with my mates dad, we're not going far
I'd be home very early if I borrowed your car.

The car's out of petrol dad, it's not very funny
I'll fill it with petrol, if you lend me some money.

Dad, now I've left home and have my own place
There's lots of odd jobs that I cannot face.

I've done my best dad, but oh what a caper
Dad, can you help me to hang this wallpaper?

The water pipe's leaking, there's lots of small pools
You're welcome to pop round dad, oh, bring your tools.

Dads don't expect payment, dads rarely get thanks
They get used and abused and treated like banks.

I never gave thought to just how much dads do
Until one fine day, I became a dad too.

And as I grow older I hope that I'll be
Just half of the dad my dad's been to me.

Robert Ilsley

A DAD

In my younger days, a dad went out to work,
he the breadwinner, mum did housework.
Dad also drove a car,
for journey near and far.
Swimming at local outdoor pool,
or at the seaside, sea was 'cool'.
At the work's allotment, gardening,
or wildlife walk, discovering.
A good natured argument about religion,
or even if that pigeon *was* a pigeon!
A dad might smoke, but tell you not to,
a dad knew best, who was who;
encouraged reading, to broaden one's mind,
even liked the marmalade's rind!
Photography, games including table tennis,
brought out the angel and even the menace!
A dad was protection, kind but strict,
kept chimney swept and deserved respect.
A dad is a person, does what he thinks best,
often there with answers, through life's quest.
So on Father's Day, remember a dad,
he may be alive, a pal
or a memory, but a dad is still a dad.

Anita Fellowes

DEAR DADDY

Father dear, I love you
I was your heart's delight
Our few years spent together
Beamed with radiant light

Daddy, you were to me
My hero, my knight, my all
Unique, the one and only
Father of fathers, your role

You cried, when I visited the dentist
You cried, when mum brushed my hair
You cried, whenever I cried
Your bond was rarer than rare

My young years, spent at your bedside
Thinking, this was our life together
The joy of the letters you wrote me
I knew you loved me forever

I have missed you for so many years
But your love, lingers on inside me
I know you watch me, day and night
What had to be, had to be

I remember your last words to me
You said, take care of your mother.
I saw your face, for the very last time
That look belonged to no other

Dear daddy, we shall never part
Your star shines bright in the sky
I was always the twinkle in your eye
Your sparkle, gets me by.

Margaret Hazard

TO DAD

To dad, my loyal companion,
My teacher and my friend -
Who whenever there's a problem,
Always has a hand to lend.
The shoulder that I lean upon,
Whenever things go wrong.
The one who taught me how to live,
to learn, and to be strong.
The voice that is my conscience,
that overwhelms me with advice,
But never says 'I told you so . . .',
If I run into strife.
Nothing matches the bond between us.
The world can throw at me what it will,
But with my father by my side,
I will keep on going still.
We have lasted through the laughter,
And the tears when times are bad,
For together we're unstoppable,
A daughter and her dad!
And so together we grow older,
And when it is my turn,
To parent someone like myself,
From you I will have learned.
So thanks for what you've made me -
A wise mind and smiling face,
That's why it's you who for eternity,
In my heart has pride of place.

Jo-anna Wesson

FLIGHT OF THOUGHT

He sits there rocking in the wooden chair,
his brow is furrowed, and his eyes do stare,
suddenly and intently a smile does appear,
upon that wind-beaten weathered face, so near.

His pipe, it puffs out smoke and smell,
as his memories pass, of pleasure and hell.
In days of youth and fair maids he knew,
and of days in war, when he 'was one of the few'.

'Tis times like this, when memories fly,
that acknowledgement of character, are there to espy.
But try as one can to lever a story,
a reply rings out, 'Ach, away ye young Tory'.

The father figure is in full splendour,
spruced up in medals for a 'reunion bender'.
When battles of old are flown and refought,
where strength and honour, were not easily bought.

That rocking chair is the central piece,
to authority, position, of a happy family niche.
Our father's place; a place of no strife.
For we know of his love of country and family life.

Alan Noble

DADS

Dads sit in chairs like big teddy bears,
   They drink cups of tea and shout at mummy,
They watch the races,
   And fiddle with their braces,
But while we play,
   They work all day.

Karen Waite (11)

BILL

He wasn't really handsome,
in stature rather small,
but to his child a special man,
the greatest dad of all.

Soft grey eyes would twinkle,
firm voice was calm and kind,
and when my fears I told to him,
comfort I would find.

Thoughtful, caring, generous too,
helping those he could,
he always made the best of things,
and tried to see the good.

Though hard he fought the battle,
on life he lost his hold,
and left this world at fifty-four,
which wasn't very old.

A teenage girl, I missed him so,
my heart was slow to mend,
not only was he dearest dad,
he was my loyal friend.

I'm proud to be his daughter,
that gentle man named Bill,
I loved him all that time ago,
today I love him still.

The years have gone by quickly,
I'm older now than he,
but all the while my dad is near,
for he's a part of me.

Avis Ciceri

DADDY'S GIRL

W e had the best dad in the world,
A quiet, unassuming man
L ike any ordinary bloke;
T o us, though, he was Superman.
E motions, not one to display,
R arely his feelings he'd convey.

E ven though he'd come home tired,
D ad would always join our game;
W as number one in our esteem,
A lthough he held no claim to fame.
R eflecting on his gentle ways
D ims my eyes in tearful haze.

H ow I recall the piggy-backs
A s we'd head home from picture shows,
R escuing me from tired legs,
R aising me up above the snows.
I loved to be his 'daddy's girl',
S afe in my heart the flame still glows.
O f all the dads in this wide world
N one was more loved by his little girl.

Kay Spurr

DEAR FATHER

Father, when I think of you
That sense of loss still fills me.
Nothing can replace you
            or the tenderness you gave me.

You were always there,
A shoulder to cry on,
Someone to rely on,
Always a helping hand
Someone to understand.

A heart full of love
With warmth enclosed me
A mind full of pride,
Not deserved by me.

Father, when I think of you,
Sometimes a child I long to be,
Safe in your security.

Joan Scarisbrick

HEAVENLY MESSAGE

For forty years
We've missed you dad,
I see mam's face
When it looks sad,
I know how much
She misses you,
I wish that
I could help,
To ease the pain
And comfort her,
I do my best
It's true,
But nothing, and
No-one ever,
Will take the place
Of you.

Joan Farlow

DADDY'S LITTLE GIRL

You told your little girl,
What was right,
What was wrong.
You knew best all along.

You taught your little girl,
What to think,
What to say.
What to do from day to day.

You showed your little girl,
What was happy,
What was sad.
To be prepared for good and bad.

You saw your little girl,
Grow into woman,
Grow her own mind.
Independently, her way to find.

You let go of your little girl,
The mould broken,
Self unfurl.
I'm no longer daddy's little girl.

Lee Brewin

MY TWO FATHERS

I want to thank you daddy
For everything you've done
You've helped me when I've needed it
Through laughter, pain and fun

From cradle to the grave
You'll always be with me
Both I really love
But one has set me free

One in heaven
One on earth
Both to me like diamonds worth
More precious than silver
More precious than gold
One is everlasting
The other's getting old!

Mark Tann

MY DAD IN A MILLION

If I look back to my childhood days,
One person stands out in so many ways.
The man who loved and comforted me when sad,
A man in a million, the number one dad.

I never really told him how much he meant,
When every single day together we spent.
He taught me the difference between wrong and right,
He read me stories each and every night.

Remembering how I learnt to ride my bike, his face I see,
Thinking about the time when I sat upon his knee.
Wondering how I learnt to read and write,
I see my dad's face shining bright.

Remembering who helped me with my sums,
I think of a man who is my best chum.
He loves me, he cares for me, he is the best,
My dad is the greatest, you can keep the rest.

It's time to thank, my best dad,
Who always loves me, and makes me laugh when sad.
I'll continue to thank him for eternity,
He is the best dad, there ever will be.

Sarah Walters

REGRETS

I remember dad, but in my heart I feel so sad
When I recall the time we shared
I never said how much I cared
He talked of war and guns so loud
His horse of which he was so proud
But all that happened long ago
I did not really want to know
For I was young and wars were past
And time was going much too fast.

I remember dad, lots of people in the ward
How could I ever have been bored
With this old man, so sweet and mild
Who loved me so his only child,
Eyes once so blue are closing now
I choked back tears, I don't know how
I whispered love, he could not hear
Then sister said 'He's gone my dear'.

Tell your dad you love him.

Roma Court

THE OTHER MAN IN MY LIFE

My wonderful husband's the man that I love
I'm sure he was sent from heaven above.
He fills my life with happiness
I love him more than words express.

But there is another man in my life
Though he already has a wife.
I'm sure she knows just how I feel
But my love for him, is so real.

He really is a marvellous man
I see him as often as I can.
He's kind, he's caring, he's handsome too
I know he'll never be untrue.

I love this man so very much
He comforts me, with his soft touch.
His tender kiss, his loving smile
I'll see him in a little while.

I bet you're wondering, who's this man?
Who gives me all the love he can.
Who cares for me, when my heart's sad
He is none other than my dad!

Sheila With The Golden Hair

THE QUIET MAN

My dad was a quiet man,
My dad seemed quite tall;
Patience was his virtue
When I was very small.
He'd sit beside me when in bed
And in soft oil lamp glow,
When measles reared its ugly head
He'd give a shadow show.
A country fellow born and bred
Next door to the Prince of Wales.
When eyebrows raised he laughed and said
'The pub at Besthorpe, that one never fails'.
Tailoring was his true trade,
He sewed for rich and famous;
High class work, but low class paid
The hours he worked, tremendous.
Sometimes he'd speak of First World War,
Like feeding children locust beans;
Never the horrors that he saw,
Only the funny bits between.
(Sapper in the Royal Engineers
Doing running repairs on a sewing machine)
My two sons gave him lots of joy,
We were all daughters - three.
Dad had always wanted a boy
But that was not to be.
My dad was a quiet man
With age his stature smaller,
But this patient, humorous, gentle man
In my heart had grown much taller.

Margaret Simmons

158

MY DAD: JIM 1912 - 1987

My daddy was a drummer
Showed me how to 'roll'
Urged me to smile when sad
Taught me all I know.

By day he fitted tools and plied
The cutlery trade he knew
By night 'on stage' in bow tie smart
The dancers' hearts he'd woo.

The bathroom was his each 'playing' night
Hair Brylcreamed shiny black
Shoes he polished mirror bright
Over the dress suit - old white mac.

To class for ballet, ballroom or tap
Through Hillsborough Park we'd go
My dad danced too as he had the view
That on stage he'd give a show.

On Sunday morns he'd make a stew
Of tripe and bacon slices.
For tea we'd dress a crab or two
With salt and peppery spices.

On stormy nights he'd take me out
On the balcony to see
The types of lightning, kind of cloud
That fascinated me.

My dad was kind to many
Always a friend it seems
I cried when he died last summer
By a tree in his 'garden of dreams'.

Avrille Oxley McCann

DAD

Dad we miss you every day
though do remember things you'd say,
Precious memories safely stored
deep in our hearts you're still adored.

Through both the good times and the bad
you'd be there and weren't we glad.
On your shoulder securely rest
your strength to give - only the best.

Folk as you not easy to find -
patient, honest and very kind.
In work and play we'd have some fun
helping others 'til all chores done.

Alas your life on earth was short
giving so much gentle support
Still sharing all our thoughts with you
for you're with us whate'er we do.

Together we will always be
happiness there for all to see.
A father and a special friend
our love for whom will never end.

Margaret Jackson

DAD'S LEGACY

The slender spire is outlined clear above the hill
Where village school stands, clustered 'neath its spell.
Here is the place where people, long since dead,
Were taught to pray; where children walked with God,
Where simple folk gave all they knew in thanks.

Inside the grey stone walls are carvings cut with loving care,
A gilded reredos and candlesticks, sanctified, blessed;
Work of a gentle man, who loved his bees
And flowers and tiny helpless things.
He asked no more.

I knew him well, and watched his reddened, work-worn hands
Make beauty for the Lord.
It was his way, the best way that he knew to offer thanks.
His grave lies near, beside his lifelong love,
Marked by a simple stone, humble and unproclaimed,
As was his wish, this patient man who wrought.

Ivy Broomfield

WHY FATHER'S DAY?

You have to have a licence to drive, or fly,
Even to live, and also to die.
Yet to be a father no licence you need.
It matters not, your colour race or creed.

Most males can become a dad,
Don't you think that rather bad?
How did you get lumbered in this way?
With this guy over whom you had no say.

Suppose your mother was to blame
For playing at love's old sweet game,
Not heeding her parents words and fears,
Saying she knew better than her peers.

Going and falling for this lad,
So now it's 'Happy Father's Day dad'.

George Bailey

MY FATHER - THE MAN FROM STONEY FALLS

My father sits deep in his armchair
        with years three score and ten.
The slow sands of our history
        sink like roots deep into my mind.
Your face aged and thoughtful
        your eyes warm and gentle.

In a flash I see your hands
        firm and strong around my shoulders
You worked the land with steel and stone
        and laid it in neat and patterned lines.

Sods rolled back in perfect curves
As sweated horses pulled and strained
        in quiet concentration
You steered the reins and head rig
        just as you showed me in my youth.

And now in this noisy room
We sit and watch your children's children at play
        and think of seasons' unrepentant rise and fall
And God's gift of creation
        to man and all.

John McLaughlin

MY FATHER

He was the inspiration in my life,
The stable factor in a fragile world;
The values I have clung to all my days
Are those he taught me, in my childhood years;
The disciplines which help me to survive
Are those he practised to the very end;
The love he gave to family and friends
Is that same love that I have tried to give
To those who need from me, what he could give.

What I am now is all because of him;
His influence in everything I've done
Is what has helped to make me what I am;
And though the principles I cherish in his name
May not be recognised by all whose lives I touch,
Within myself, I know that what is good
In all I try to do, is due to him;
For his example guides my every thought,
And knowing that, I fear not what I do.

So, 'tho he's gone, he lives on still in me.
My father.

Jean Scott

FROM DAD TO GRANDAD

Daddy, where have the years gone?
The years you taught me right from wrong.
Daddy's girl, your pride and joy,
Always buying me presents, a book or a toy.
You were my hero, my shining knight,
If I was in trouble you made things right.
It's been thirty years since you became my dad,
And now I have made you a proud grandad.
Now all the things you did for me,
You do for my children, all three.
Your face is now covered with line after line,
As I watch you give them what was once mine.
I love you dad with all my heart,
Even though we've grown apart.
I know one day this earth you'll leave,
And I'll be left behind to grieve.
I pray that day is far away,
And you'll still be here when you're old and grey.
Believe me dad what I say is true,
I will always love you.

Dawn Kerr

TRIBUTE TO DAD

Long ago when I was young
Dear dad was always there
Would come in from the garden
With treats of plum or pear

Dad was a very quiet man
Gentle kind and good
He always worked so very hard
And did the best he could

We all went for walks in the country
Where the swallows flew high in the sky
When my little legs were tired
I rode on dad's shoulders so high

Sometimes we went for a bike ride
Through the lovely countryside
Birds singing in the treetops
Underneath shy rabbits hide

Although dad now lives with the angels
I can still feel him close by my side
Especially when I'm in the country
Under trees where shy rabbits hide

Angela Pearson

MO'S DAD
(Dedicated to the memory of my friend Maureen Franklin's dad)

I recall him in his garden,
He tended it with care,
The seasons came and lengthened,
But yet he lingered there.
Of all the fathers I have met
He seemed the dearest dad
So gentle, kind and helpful,
He always made one glad.

He's free now from his care and pain,
But the birds he loved still sing
For life must still go on for us,
Like the flowers that bloom each spring.
Think of him in his garden,
Remember him with love
And that his gentle loving hands
Tend God's garden up above.

Joan Heybourn

GOODBYE DAD

We never really sat down,
and said the things we felt,
until those gloomy winter days,
when snow began to melt,
by then I had been blessed with children,
just as you Dad, long ago had been,
so many hidden things in life,
you spoke of, I now have seen,
a wicked twist of destiny took you away too soon,
surviving operations, too weak to hold a spoon,
slowly growing stronger, within, a hidden mass,
to re-emerge and take your life, consign you to the past,
I held your hand helplessly, and watched the tears fall,
down a timeless face with laughter lines,
no laughter now at all.
You saw me come into this world, loved me all my life,
supported me through failure and success, saw me take a wife,
now I see the tears you weep, as raindrops from the sky,
too weak to wipe them all away, too tired to even try.
I miss you Dad, I always will, I look for you each day,
maybe when I too join you,
this is what my son might say.

Pat Judson

MY IDEAL MAN

My ideal man is strong
but sometimes needs me.
My ideal man has faith in me
to follow -
And support me.
My ideal man can share
the laughter and tears.
My ideal man chastises
for he knows better by years.
My ideal man goes his own way
And lets me go mine.
He listens when I need him,
For me, has always time.
My ideal man would die for me,
Sacrifice all, freely
Give, and ask nothing in return,
Is a teacher, but always humble
enough to learn,
Comforts me when I'm sad
Holds no grudges if I'm bad.
The one who never lets me down
Thinks of me when I'm not around
And when I see him, he's always glad
My ideal man, is (of course) my *dad!*

Andrea S Thomas

MY DAD

In Dorset all his life was spent,
To foreign lands he never went;
Cows and calves for him his life,
He loved each one, as did his wife.

Through First World War he walked to school,
The Lady Head she was so cool;
Respect she gained from all the class,
I loved his tales of days long past.

A full day's work at fourteen years,
With cows and horses but no fears;
His Dad one lunchtime fell asleep,
For only son his task was deep.

From early morn till time to lock,
He gave his life to land and stock;
To milk, to thatch, to hedge, to sow,
His skill and talents all on show.

Throughout my childhood help was great,
With praise, support and real debate;
At sport he loved to bowl at cricket,
He taught me well to fend my wickets.

He served his king in Second World War,
His leadership sought by more and more;
He managed farm for thirty years,
Till all was sold he shed no tears.

Retirement plans were all in hand,
With bungalow built on gifted land;
The welcome feast ne'er went ahead,
For night before Dad dropped down dead.

John Paulley

PICTURES OF DAD

So many pictures of you Dad,
I don't know where to start.
So many precious memories
Printed on my heart . . .
Lighting up your cigarette
In photo debonair,
Teaching me, 'That Great Big Cake'
On the wicker chair,
Singing songs that Jolson sang
Still running through my mind,
Pushing me on the swings
When we went to Glynde,
Waving to me on your bike
When I came home for lunch,
Bringing us bags of sweets
On Saturdays to munch,
Always make us laugh
Telling Max Miller jokes,
Taking us to C & A
To buy our winter coats,
Always working hard for me
Every single day,
Working long hours overtime
So at school I'd stay.
So many pictures of you dad,
In each one I recall
You are the best Dad in the world,
The dearest of them all.

Jenny Hall

MY HERO

He was not a man of action;
His words were few but wise,
And in my pre-school days
He was a hero in my eyes.

And then in the school playground
The children at their play
Said, 'My dad's younger than your dad',
And then, they'd run away.

'And my dad's taller than your dad.'
I went home and it was true.
I stood with hands on hips
and said, 'I don't think I like you'.

But when I told him why
I did not like him anymore,
He quietly and slowly
Walked across the floor.

He put his hands upon my shoulders,
In his eyes, no sense of failure,
'Tell them I was six feet tall
Until I walked home from Australia'.

My hero lived again;
And I rushed out to tell them all,
That my old and very small dad
Was really six feet tall.

In later years, the penny dropped
And how we laughed about it.
I told him, 'You're my hero'.
And at no time did I doubt it.

Billy Baird

FATHER

All I can say of my dad is bad,
It's very sad.
From my earliest impressions
He hated his relations,
Brother, father, step-mother too
Male in-laws fits of jealousy he threw.
'His Father' by Victorian Silas Hocking
He read to me at night. It was shocking.
'Please don't read any more' my mother said.
For nightmares it gave me but still on he read.
An attack of asthma was 'giving way'
He locked the door so out I must stay.
Mum could see no wrong in Harry
A second chance and the same man she'd marry.
I was the one that was not wanted
But must excel, so education was granted,
To be a clever daughter, as *he'd* made me
To be introduced, for all the world to see
How he'd trained the 'gifts' he'd passed on
Responsible for my success, he was the one.
Love he had for three women only.
In child-birth his mother had left him lonely
My grandma who left him soon after my birth,
And my mum. He said I'd caused her death.
Escaping to my young auntie's whenever I was able.
In his 90th year he still had his feet under my table.

Alice Hall

MY DAD

There's one thing I've always had
This precious person I call my dad,
He helped to create me,
He gave me a life,
Never gets on my case or gives me strife
He's always in my heart and deep within -
my mind,
He's a special person the caring kind
I know not to trust any old lad,
There's only one man I trust and that's *my dad.*

Kieghley Joyce

THE DAILY BUZZ

What's the weather like with you?
My barometer's falling too.
How's the gout, no pain today?
Perhaps the rain will stay away.
Tomatoes coming on a treat,
When they're ripe you'll feed the street.
I'm off to Crete again in May.
You'll feed my fish while I'm away?
The dog, oh yes, she'd love to stay,
She'll get long walks and lots of play.
How's mum's throat? It's getting better,
Has she finished Sarah's sweater?
Have you done today's crossword?
Ten across I've never heard.
You think it is an anagram,
You've just had egg with chips and ham.
Did auntie Sue give you a call?
We never hear from her at all.
Have you ten pounds that I could borrow?
Oh, all right dad, I'll ring tomorrow!

Mary Cooper

171

UNSPOKEN WORDS

I wish that I had told you dad
More often than I did
How very much I loved you
When I was just a kid

If I could write a book
Of my childhood spent with you
I would fill each page with memories
And the love I had for you.

I remember dad when I was young
How I'd sit upon your knee.
Where I would ride a galloping horse
That would jump at the count of three

I remember too the walks we had
When dressed in our Sunday best
Trying not to dirty
The dress that had just been pressed

We'd walk across the meadows
Or down a country lane
Stop and pick some flowers
And make a daisy chain

I treasure all these memories
Whenever I think of you
And though the words weren't spoken
I really did love you

Margaret L Hawkins

A POEM FOR DAD

What gratitude I owe to thee
The dad who gave up all for me
Now deep is calling unto deep
Lord, his precious soul to keep

You gave me happiness untold
Kept me brave and made me bold
When I relive those carefree days,
It is with joy I sing your praise

Cuddly pets and green green fields
How rich our orchards' juicy yields
Fine clothes and food and warmth supplied
There was naught I was denied

Ne'er once heard you e'er complain
You hid your hurts - concealed the pain
I'd not have known your acts of war
But for the cruel scars you bore

A kindly man in word and deeds
Right conscious of another's needs
I love to remember this dad of mine
Who made childhood days so divine

Norah Page

FOR A SPECIAL DAD ON FATHER'S DAY

Today is special
in every single way

Because today
it's Father's Day

See the difference in the world
with you here

With you standing beside us we've
got no fear

So enjoy this day dear father
it only happens once a year

So let's celebrate Father's Day
with a great big loud cheer!

Shakira Khanom (12)

YOU'RE GONE

Oh how I wish I could see you again
You cared and loved us so very much
From being small to growing up
You were there to help us through
Dad I miss you so very much
My heart broke when you went
Not to leave us, God called your name
An emptiness you left no one can fill
Memories I hold so dear

No make-up you said it will spoil your skin
Boys who you didn't like us to have
You chased them away
No one seemed good enough did they

Your grandchildren you would have loved so much
I tell them how soft and sensitive you were
How kind and gentle like a gentle giant
You suffered from having too big a heart
So God called you so you hurt no more
I hurt dad because you're not here
Maybe soon we will meet again
As no one can ever replace you

Evelyn Farr

DEAR DAD

Even though you left me
You have always been near
If I'm ever in trouble
You have made things so crystal clear

I tell you everything about my life
And in which direction it turns
You accept me for who I am
And there's one thing I've learned

With you being so far away and out of reach
I have to find other ways to show you I care.
Phoning and writing is one way
But I'd rather have you here next to me

So you can hold me when I'm blue
And have a shoulder to cry on
But saying this I know wherever you are
You love me and daddy I love you too

I shall love you for eternity
Because you mean so very much to me.

Nadia Darwish

THIS WAS MY POP

We never called him father
And daddy was all slop
The name we kids all called him
Was short and simple, Pop.

He was a walking fashion plate
With spats and smart cravat
And never went outside the house
Without his bowler hat.

Sometimes on a Saturday
While playing with my top
The other boys would whisper, Joe
Hey up, here comes your Pop.

I'd look up at him standing there
Just leaning on his stick
Want to come up West, he'd say
I'm beside him double quick.

The East End of the thirties
Left little room for pride
But I was always proud to be
Walking by his side.

All that's left is a marble slab
To show where Pop's life ended
But he left a place deep in my heart
That never can be mended.

Joe Silver

PORTRAIT

To my children he's Grandpa, seventy today,
Who comes on a visit from far away,
Driving a car which is getting old
Just like he is - or that's what he's told!

Unpaid chauffeur and odd job man,
He does the chores that no-one else can,
Hands over his pension to buy the kids sweets
And takes them walking through winter streets.

He races around on Grannie's heels,
Down the M1 on ageing wheels
To Scotland, Canada, the Isle of Wight,
Up from his bed in the middle of the night.

You may think, if you look at him now,
That he's getting old, there's grey at his brow;
To his four grandchildren he's old as the sky
And Grannie sees youth slipped too quickly by;

But to me, all these years and he's never changed;
I've grown up and my life's rearranged
But he's still there in the same old place,
There to go back to, that well-loved face;
Not a day older, it seems to me,
Than he was when I sat on my Daddy's knee.

Val Sutton

NEVER LOVED

My childhood wasn't a happy one,
It was very rare my father would come,
To take me by the hand, and play with me,
He would sit, and just watch TV,
I'd hurt my hand, no magic kiss,
To make it better, couldn't bother with this,
Wouldn't hold my hand, walking down the streets,
To shut me up, he'd give me a bag of sweets,
Not ever sitting, on his knee,
Like most little girls do frequently,
Usually dad's little ray of sunshine,
That never happened, unfortunately with mine,
The goodnight kiss, I never had,
Or the goodnight wish from my dad,
Hugs and kisses, what were they,
From my dad, never came my way,
The strange thing was, I loved him so,
The love for me, he never showed,
I always wished that he could,
One day love me as he should,
I was always jealous of my friends,
With their fathers time they'd spend,
The hugs and kisses I'd see them get,
Full of envy and regret,
But now I'm older, things stayed the same,
My father's rejection, caused me pain,
He'll never change, to his dying day,
I love you was what I wanted him to say.

Lynn Hallifax

THE FOUNDATIONS OF LIFE

I remember you helping me do my sums
the teacher was not pleased
as we got them all wrong.
I remember you being proud
and would compliment me very loud
on my new taffeta party dresses.
You brushed my long hair
and didn't think it very fair
when you had to tie it up with bows of ribbon.
I remember in a storm
on your bike you arrived, to take me home
so afraid that I was alone
but we were safe sheltering in a shop.
Of your garden you were proud
and a corner you allowed
me to grow some plants and seeds
but I never inherited your green fingers.
Each day I smile and sing
and hope my love will wing
its way upwards to heaven to you.
I remember the foundations of life
of love and laughter you taught me.
I can garden, paint and read a book
but a woman's place is in the home
and I somehow never learned to cook.
I remember you and pray
for the privilege of having you as a father
and say - *thank you.*

Rosemary Medland

DAD ME AND THE TWO FIFTY TWIN

I was sitting about I had nothing to do
In my daydreams dad I saw pictures of you
They were so long ago thirty years maybe more
If my mind serves me right I was just three or four
You washed me and dressed me and tied my shoe laces
Together we set off for the motorbike races
In your black Mark Ten Jag with its big steering wheel
You were never to know how important I'd feel
Whenever you said without even a grin
That one day I would race a two fifty twin
It was right there and then that I must have been smitten
By the motorcycling bug and once you are bitten
There is no turning back you're there year in year out
With a great dedication that is never in doubt
Our finance was such that I never did ride
The two fifty twin that was your greatest pride
Instead I'm a marshal and I run my own zone
And even though I'm grown up I don't go alone
Our roles are reversed now it's me that takes you
If it weren't for the racing we'd have nothing to do
The adrenaline still flows when they are flat on their tanks
So for my interest in bikes dad I'll say a big thanks

David Gibbons

DADDY'S LITTLE GIRL

They say that I'm Daddy's little girl
     But I don't care.
I'm proud of him you know
     I suppose I shouldn't boast so.
He has always cared for me
     Bringing me up to love you see,
My daddy means the world to me.

He has worked hard for what he's got
And really deserves the lot.
Back when he was a boy
He didn't even have a toy.
Life was hard then you see
But now my daddy has got me.
I love my daddy you see.

Sharon Irwin

A TRIBUTE TO DAD

When asked to write for Father's Day
I didn't know what I could say
My dad he died at 64
That seemed the end there was no more
And then my mind in time went back
To life along the *beaten track.*

Dad was just an ordinary chap
But when I sat upon his lap
I was his princess, he was my king
My dad to me was *everything.*

He was a coal-miner in the cold damp earth
So he knew what life was worth
He taught his children right from wrong
And often entertained us with a song.

Dad cared for others all his life
No matter what the stress or strife
Sharing with others whatever he had
We really loved our *dear old dad . . .*

Hilda Mary Regan

A TEAR FOR EACH MEMORY

Stretching my mind back to days of joy,
I remember them well I was a very young boy
My mother and father myself and the boys
Would prepare for our picnic and seek peace from the noise.
With sandwiches and cakes and a big flask of tea
We would set off on our journey to a place called Roche
Abbey.
A much loved beauty spot where monks used to
Reside.
Its famous old ruins stand proud in the air
And it's lovely to visit to reminisce of the past
About our weekly walked journey where fun and joy
Were cast.
And I know in my heart if our dear dad was still
With us, we would all go again
This is but one little memory that will always remain.

Trevor Barnes

MISSING DAD

As you walk the path to the next world Dad
We hope that you will find
A little time to spare a thought
For the ones you've left behind

There's no-one who could take your place
As you're one of a kind
So you'll always be here with us Dad
For you're locked here in our minds

We know you're resting now in peace
And know you're happy too
But we love you and we miss you
As we are a part of you.

E Waller

MY DAD

My dad is just the greatest friend a daughter ever had.
He's silly when he wants to be but serious when you're bad.
I remember all our childhood days the fun we used to have.
Even all those early calls on April fools we've had.

I think of all those winter days we stood out in the garden.
First you gave us cod liver oil and then you did us pardon.
I'm off to get the treacle next I'll be a little while, now
you just stay right where you are you whispered with a smile.
Then you would come and pat our backs and say it's good for
you, we must admit we never ever suffered with the flu.

You built us all a great big swing made from two big trees,
what a great achievement you made it with such ease. It lasted
us for many years we nearly wore it out. But then we had to
leave it as we moved to our new house.

So when you're feeling lonely dad, and we know you sometimes do
and you look back upon your life this is what you do remember
all those special times that we all spent with you.

Christine Licence

MY DADDY

My daddy is a tall man
Well tall compared to me.
His hair is grey, he's going bald
But he's beautiful to me.

He's always there when I need him
He wipes away my fears.
There's no-one like my daddy
He's always in my prayers.
I love you Daddy.

Kate Crawford

HIS STYLE

If my dad was alive today,
would he say he was proud of me?
It's taken me so long to know
how proud of him I'll always be.

I was quite a difficult child,
a stubborn and rebellious youth;
To get out of a scrape I'd lie
and swear to dad it was the truth.

He sent me to quite a grand school,
which stood in spacious grounds with trees,
My dad worked nights as well as days
to help pay the enormous fees.

One day I decided to leave:
at home I couldn't stay out late.
Freedom at last, how great I thought,
my dad said he wished I would wait.

I ignored the look in his eyes,
his little girl was leaving home;
Unharnessed youth with spite can wound
when adolescents want to roam.

Of course, my dad was on my side,
he wanted just the best for me,
I regret the pain I caused him,
he hid it well, I didn't see.

I won't forget my super dad,
his loving eyes and happy smile,
Although he's no longer in my world,
I try to follow in his style.

Mary Care

DAD

(for my father Ronald Broadbent
who celebrated his 70th birthday on 1st December 1996)

I remember vividly, when as a child upon your knee,
You'd tell me of the fun you'd had, when you yourself were just a lad.
You'd tell me how you used to play cowboys and Indians every day,
You'd run as though upon a horse. You had the fastest one of course.
And I remember later on, the parties that were so much fun,
With aunties, uncles, cousins too, your family meant a lot to you.
You'd play your records from the war and some I think were from before,
You weren't too keen on modern songs, but how I loved those singalongs.
I recall when summer came, you'd often like to play a game,
Of cricket in the local park. We'd play all day till it got dark.
Our holidays always the same, we'd travel England on a train,
You wouldn't fly, you wouldn't sail, but you *did* work for British Rail.
Thinking back to Christmas Eve, as children you helped us believe,
You'd ring a bell and then you'd say that it was Santa on his sleigh.
You'd hire a book, always the same, A Christmas Carol was its name,
You'd read it to us every night, it made my Christmas seem just right.
December 1st is a special occasion, it's time for a family celebration,
For you'll be 70 on that day, and I'd like to take this chance to say,
Although I've grown up and left home and have a daughter of my own,
I'd like to thank you for the years, filled with laughter, love and tears.
And tell you just how proud I am, of you my dad, a special man,
A man so good, so kind and true,
Happy birthday dad. I love you.

Sandra Rowland

HIMSELF

There's just no doubt
You're the world's best dad
Never be a better dad it's true

I can only humbly try to describe
What it's like
To even have a dad like you

You're a man among men
A tower of strength
So subtle and debonair

Obviously bred from royal stock
You've got that aloof air

Gifted, charming, witty
One of the boys
Where you stand is sacred ground

Worshipped by men and women alike
Your charisma just abounds

OK so I get carried away
You're just a normal dad

But you'll always be
One in a million to me
And life without you would be sad.

Fred Tighe

MY DEAR OLD DAD IN HIS 90TH YEAR 1995

Harry, my dad, is a character -
Of that there is no doubt!
In May he went into hospital
But proved he knew what life is all about . . .
His knowledge built over almost ninety years
Proves stability for sure -
He is never short of stories
For patients present found a new cure!
One commented loud and clear
'No entertainment tax required while Harry is in here!'

Devoted visitors thought they knew best
Saying 'Make the most of convalescence'
You need more time to rest -
Bourton Cottage Hospital . . . a lovely place to be . . .
Stay there another week.
But 'Home as soon as possible!' said he!
My dad is far from meek
Alice, eighty-nine years, will look after me.

Alas! A week went by . . .
Then such a shock for him -
Alice had a stroke, who knows why?
They are so both determined it isn't true -
Dad visiting her each day . . .
Now what could we do?
We all thought Alice would never be the same
But she fought through
And back home to dad she came
Only one year younger . . in time for his 90th party too.

A J Hambling

A VISIT FROM MY FATHER

(Dedicated to Ted Gardner Dec 27 1914 - Mar 26 1996)

My father came and spoke with me
In riddles and rhymes,
And cryptic verse
Those muddled stanzas I couldn't discern
Yet somehow his message,
Was exactingly terse.

His features once obvious
A mere few days before,
Were hard to define, confusing, distorted
He lent across and kissed my brow
Something to which,
He had never resorted.

He gestured in parting
As if to convey,
Tell everyone Michael
You know why I'm here
I've come to set your mind at rest,
To ease your conscience and allay all fear.

For come the morning
This dream will be gone
And the tears you part
Will be our blesséd song
So use the gift of life with joy,
We will all be wiser when we meet, anon.

Michael Gardner

DAD

Taciturn, tolerant, tidy,
Sensitive, soulful and stern:
From your wealth of character's riches
As a child I had so much to learn.

As a child I admit I was wary,
Fearing God's wrath, who knows what if I strayed.
Yet nevertheless sought your friendship
Through the years as I learnt whilst I played.

It was only when very much older
I discovered your humour and fun.
I guess I would have taken advantage
If I'd discovered them whilst I was young.

When work made your absence essential
You returned, having never lost touch,
Finding sanctuary, solace and substance
In the garden you cherished so much.

And there, midst sweet fruits and bright blossom
Side by side working nature's rich soil,
We discovered exhaustion and blessing:
The wages of practical toil.

You're a man of philosophy, spirit,
Though you rarely are found in a pew.
I met God in the peace of your garden,
Through your garden I came to know you.

Linda M Jones

MY DAD

Always kind and always fair
Always helpful, always there
Always giving good advice
That's my dad, so fine and nice

Often cutting his big hedge
Always growing his own veg
Often smiling, telling jokes
That's my dad, a real good bloke

Never lazy, cruel or mean
Often bowling on the green
Sometimes shopping for my mum
That's my dad, a real good chum

Always there to lend a hand
Often working on his land
Sometimes cycling down the road
That's my dad, *as good as gold*

Sometimes watching garden birds
Often doing hard crosswords
Sometimes painting, whistling loud
That's my dad, so strong and proud

Always friendly, often sunny
Always generous with his money
Always likes to make things work
That's my dad, *salt of the earth!*

Jill Campbell

OUR DAD

Did we say how much we loved him
Did we show how much we cared,
Did we take his love for granted
Because we knew that he was there?

He'd leave the house before the sun
Had risen in the morning sky,
Not returning 'til the shadows
Heralded the long dark night.

But at weekends he was with us
Summer Sundays by the sea,
Playing ball games in the park
Before we all went home to tea.

How he loved to tend his garden
Growing vegetables galore,
Soft fruits trailing up the fences
Borders bright with scented flowers.

A quiet man, he didn't say much
But would listen when we talked,
A man of simple country wisdom
We had respect for what he thought.

He was strong in his affections
But didn't demonstrate his love,
He was devoted to our mother
And she returned unfailing love.

I'm sure he knew that we all loved him
Each one of his daughters three,
So many things remind us of him
In our hearts he'll always be.

Edna Cosby

OPEN LETTER

Hello Dad, it's us, your daughters here.
Don't worry we're not in trouble, have trust, never fear.
We may have grown up but we still need your help,
Can you teach us to drive, please Dad, we don't trust anyone else.

Do you remember all the things that we have done before,
You have been a great dad, and we tried your patience to the core.
We had great holidays you used to take us miles,
You would laugh and play with us, always ready with a smile

You have taught us much, about right and wrong,
Hey it's getting poetic Dad, no fret we are not going to burst into song.

As we have got older, the more I suppose you have had to worry.
We found out about boys, stayed out late, well, now we will say sorry.

You are more than a dad you are a friend.
You will advise, give an opinion, you even know the latest trends
You actually like some of the music we like to play,
That is more than some of friends' fathers can say.

Well back to the point in question, our very special friend
About the driving lessons, we cannot afford to pay, on you can we depend
If you could help us out on this small point, Dad dear Dad,
We can save all the money for a something special on Father's Day.

Christine Flory

MY HAT

Ashness Gill in its bright autumn colours,
Rosy berries on tall rowan trees.
'I'll take a photo', said dad, 'to remind us,
So stand by the waterfall, please'.

Perched on a rock amid rushing waters,
Father then snapped the full frothing fall;
Then he slipped, and down went the camera,
Dad's pom-pom beret and all!

Over the edge went the fine knitted hat,
Floating upside-down in mid-stream,
We chased after among the high bracken,
Seeking its bright yellow gleam.

Captured at last, the soggy wet bundle
Was wrung out with might and with main;
But, sad to relate, in spite of due care,
It was never the same again!

Dawn Coates

MY DAD

There used to be a list, at the top of our street,
A long time ago,
A list of names upon the wall, with flowers beneath,
Renewed from day to day,
So many names of men, some I knew, but I was very young,
Finding out as I grew,
They had all been killed in France,
All the young men of our street,
And they marched away from us - who weep,
Moms and dads, little lads, sweethearts, babs and friends,
They went away from me with webbing on their feet,
And through the years it stayed,
This list at the top of our street,
Then they demolished it, the road and houses all,
But now as I grow older, and I think of all the life I've had,
Never will I forget, the lost life of *my dad*.

Joan McAvoy

DADDY

Nights filled with song and laughter sitting round the fire.
Daddy's in his armchair, playing his guitar.
Dressed in our pyjamas we sing out sweet and loud.
And gazing up into his face he looks so very proud.

The house is warm and friendly, a smile on every face.
The wind it is a howling, but it's not heard in this place.
For his music fills the air and his eyes just seem to say,
That your daddy loves you all so much he'll never go away.

We're yawning but we're fighting the sleep that fills our eyes.
The four of us are nodding off as darkness fills the skies,
But his strong arms lift us gently and for a moment holds us tight,
As he carries us to bed and kisses us goodnight.

I can't put down in words all the love and joy we shared.
It would take forever and a day to show how much he cared.
For everyone has a daddy but my daddy is special to me,
For his love just keeps on growing, and it's there for all to see.

So Daddy when I think of you it's music that I hear.
For you always seemed to sing your love out loud and very clear.
And I know you hold this picture like I do tonight,
When we sat in our pyjamas and you held us all so tight.

Tanya Fisher

POEMS FOR DADDY

I have a loving daddy
Who is very good to me.
He gives me lots of goodies,
And takes me out to tea.

He is my person special,
Who tucks me up at night.
Passes me my teddybear,
Then kisses me goodnight.

He takes me to the pictures
To watch a great great show.
And I get unhappy when it's time to go.

He wipes my tears when I am sad,
He punishes me when I am bad.
But through it all I love him so
Dearest daddy don't ever go.

Mary Farr

MY FATHER

Why was he chosen
With his home, his children and his wife
He lived quite an ordinary life.
Just an ordinary man, you say,
No not that, he was noble in his way.
His eyes were green, his forehead high
He had a tender face
He taught me what I ought to know
Of principles and grace.
He was quite a placid man
But, determined too, could be
He taught me to discuss those things
On which one could not agree.
In money we were rather poor
But in spiritual things
We had much more, than most.
It was he who gave me my love of music,
To appreciate good art,
He is my darling father
He's dead, but not in my heart.

Sarah Robinson

LOVE STILL GROWING

Dad was in the army
Mum was here at home
We didn't have a telephone
So Dad he could not phone
But he really loved our mother
So wrote whene'er he could
He did it because he wanted to
And not because he should
Before dying, he said that if he could
Find a way to get in touch, he would
But up to yet, there's been no sign of him
And would like to see again his massive grin
Spreading from one ear to another
As he says 'Hello' to Mother
For he really loved our mother
They were together until the end
But he wasn't just her lover
He was also her best friend
Many years have passed now
And don't know if, or how
But Mum says that he is here
Just for her, has he managed to appear
Yes Dad I miss you too, in many different ways
Helping me through problems, laughing when in play
As I do the same things we used to share
I think of you always, imagining you are there
So although you left us, many years ago
All my love for you, still remains to grow

Margaret J Morris

POEM FOR DAD

There is a man I love so dear
He's always there for me
When I am with him there is no fear
I trust him eternally

When I was a child I would hold his hand
It was always so big and so warm
He was always there to understand
Since the day my small body was born

I would climb into bed and he'd read me a tale
Of fairies and pixies and elves
Then before very long when my eyelids fell
The book was returned to the shelves

One day I grew up and flew the nest
To a little abode of my own
But I've never loved him any less
Since the day I moved out of his home.

I've always been proud of my wonderful dad
No other could take his place
The most wonderful day I ever had
Was when I saw such warmth in his face

I walked down the aisle upon my dad's side
As family and friends looked in awe
A silent tear fell that my veil couldn't hide
As I looked at the dad I adore.

A year since has passed since he gave me away
Another man stands at my side
But I'll never forget my special day
When my dad looked at me with such pride.

Sarah-Jane Carter

ON FATHER'S DAY

We don't have much money
And gifts are so dear,
So I've written a verse
I would like you to hear:

With your cuddles and kisses you dry all my tears.
With your hugs and your laughter you wipe out my fears.
I'll grow up contented that you are my guide
To teach and protect me, as I walk by your side.
At times, though I'm naughty you try not to scold,
You remind me I'm big 'cause I'm seven years old.

I've thought of a gift now;
I won't make a din.
So slumber on Daddy
And have a lie in!

Marian Avis

FOR MY FATHER

My father was a good man, with the standards of his day.
His time was late Victorian: middle-class, and here to stay.
My education . . . disciplined, if welcomed or if not.
My home . . . secure and orderly: which means an awful lot.

He visualised his business as a service he must heed.
He did not live for profit, and was generous to need.
We took it all for granted . . . for we did not understand
How valuable these lessons are when things get out of hand.

He tried to mould his children to the lifestyle that he knew;
But he always tried to help us when we failed to follow through.
We were never close nor friendly, and this worries me a bit,
For I owe him not a little, and was not aware of it.

To call God Father is for some a signal of alarm.
Some earthly dads are shockers, and do little else but harm.
My father showed a touch of what I owe in heavenly debt.
The more I realise it, then the less I should regret.

Simon Peterson

DEAREST DAD
(Dedicated to Mr A S Jones, a very dear dad)

Dearest dad, this poem you will *never* read,
But in writing poetry you *said* I'd succeed.
You always made me so proud of *you*
How I wished you had lived,
To see *me* through.
My verses I know will make mother proud,
But my dearest wish was that you be allowed,
To live to see my poetry in print,
But as your vision dimmed, you could only squint.
Your heart gave up after many a fight,
I felt *so* helpless - I now feel I must write,
To maybe carry a part of you through,
Each day that I live, and pay my due.
If *there* is a window in heaven please look,
My dearest dad at a poetry book,
Maybe, just maybe, you will know you were dear,
And my poetry will tell you I'll *always* be near.

B H Dance

ALL ABOUT DAD

Dad you have always been near,
When I fell over, you'd say 'It's all better dear.'
Your understanding stretched pretty far,
Even when I crashed Mum's new green car!

Your work in the bank had us all on the move,
At three different schools the Sudder's did prove,
They really were a great family you see,
With Ruth, Anne, Ros, then Jen in primary three.

We enjoyed the long and breathtaking walks,
Detailed and perhaps *confusing* mathematical talks.
You held my hand in that very special way,
I remember it still to this very day.

Camping holidays were always such fun,
Up to Portsoy or to Norway's *cold sun*
You were always good at putting up the tent,
Regardless of when or where we went.

Your retirement from Shell, well what can I say?
Was indeed for us all a very special day,
Now a man of leisure all day long,
You can garden, *dig* and sing Mum's new song.

Archaeology for you is a real big delight.
You typed up those notes by day and by night.
The old pot which you pieced together,
Had evidently survived many seasons of weather.

Dad, thanks again for all you have done,
For the love you give me and 28 years of fun.
I don't say it often but I'd just like to say,
I love you and thank you for your special Dad-way.

Ruth L Ironside

TO DAD

Forty years of married life, my mother gave to you,
But, you were never faithful, never trying to be true.
Sometimes when you were angry, you would beat her to the floor,
You'd slap us children round a bit, then throw her through the door.

She stood by you, no matter what, she loved you through and through,
But you just didn't care for her, you did what you must do.
You'd have lipstick on your collar, in the morning, you'd come home,
Another sleepless night for Mum, another night alone.

I remember one cold winter, Mum came in so worn and pale,
You'd been picked up for stealing, and been given one year's jail.
The neighbours often shunned her, and she hung her head in shame,
There was no-one she could turn to, no-one to share her pain.

We children were still little, and other kids are cruel,
We were bullied something awful, every time we went to school.
The years passed by, you didn't change, you're rotten through and through
You call yourself a father, you didn't have a clue.

The only thing you gave me, not counting my poor mother,
Was a lovely older sister, one young, one older brother.
And then at last you left her, for a woman with some dough,
Can you hear the people laughing, as down the road you go.

And sometimes when I see you, around the town with her,
I really don't feel anything, it's as if you never were.
You've turned your back on everyone, and we really just don't care,
You know it's really wonderful, to know that you're not there.

Now Mum is really happy, and I'd just like you to know,
I only wish you'd left her, twenty, thirty years ago . . .

T Smith

ARE YOU WATCHING?

You were my inspiration and my guiding light.
And then the stroke came and cruelly took your sight.
In such a short time you became fragile and old
But underneath your fragility you had a heart of gold.
I admired you so and loved you true and deep
And the memories of you are in my heart to keep.
You were my dad so strong and kind
And a better person it would be hard to find.
You held me when I cried and rocked me to and fro
Why couldn't you live forever? Why did you have to go?
You see I need you now I want your love and protection
I need you to give me your fatherly affection.
But that is not to be so I'll have to go on hoping
That somehow you're watching me to make sure that I am coping.
So goodnight Dad wherever you may be
And don't forget - watch carefully over me.

Gena McCrystal

A WANTED MAN (ERNEST HUMBLE)

Our Western hero, our own John Wayne
Shenandoah, Virginian the brave Shane.
A hardworking marshall in his work and homestead.
A loving husband, father, grandpa;
By example his posse is led.

Una is his loyal partner and their gift from heaven;
Was children numbering a 'Magnificent Seven!'
Grandpa also to nine, with one on the way.
A true, respected 'Quiet Man' in life day to day.
A wanted dad the family all say
Our reward is seeing him everyday.

Patrick Humble

DEAREST DAD

My dearest dad, I'm very sad that I could never say,
How much I really loved you, though I kissed you every day.
You were my hero, tall and brave, my knight in shining
armour,
Your stories told around the fire at night were filled
with wonder.
You taught us how to care for birds and animals as well,
With you we'd share our secrets, and know you'd never
tell.
You taught us that to feel love and compassion wasn't
weak,
And then in summer taught us how to fish from off the
beach.
The love I feel, I always felt, I guess I always will,
I just wish I'd told you to your face, when you were
with us still.

Winifred Jenkins

OUR DAD

You're more than a dad you're a friend too
You're always there to lend a hand in times of trouble
You're there to dry our tears
And you're there to put away our fears
You mean a lot to me
People say you're just our step-dad because our dad is dead
But you married our mum and so then became our dad
        Although my sisters wish that you hadn't
So why can't they accept you the way I do
For now you have become our dad

Geraldine Perkins

A FATHER TRUE

The tear fell from its gentle source
to land upon the hand
Which penned the message
That he who walked upon this earth
is no longer.

He who held her hand
is no longer.
He who held her safe
is no longer.
He who kissed her cheek
is no longer.

He who once was young
is no longer.
He who intimately embraced her
touched her heart.
Kissed her lips
is no longer.

He who once did cry
Call her name
Curse her foolishness
is no longer.

He who stayed the course
proved his worth
sired his heirs
gave them pride
is no longer.
But never to be forgot.

Keith Arbie Johnson

A SPECIAL DAD

Dad was very special to me,
Was he rich you say or well known,
No just an ordinary working chap
Toiling hard for family and home.

In his younger days it has been said
A large family he helped to raise,
His stepmother, brothers and sisters
Being thankful for his kindly ways.

Eventually after Dad married
I then arrived on the scene.
Born into a nice loving home
No better could there ever have been.

When I was only a young child
Many treats he brought home for me,
How I loved to hear funny stories he told
As I sat happily on his knee.

Dad was well known in our village,
For him everyone has a kind word,
He was always ready to lend a hand
He believed a job was much better shared.

Full of fun and good humour,
A lovely smile upon his face,
All these things I remember
And will never from my memory erase.

He was a good and kind man,
My guardian and best friend,
If only I could see him now
Maybe, when the Lord for me does send.

Barbara Sowden

DAD

Remember when I was eleven years old,
you took me to my first game.
The atmosphere was so exciting,
but our team lost, what a shame.

Then the winter of sixty three,
snow lay very deep.
You built me a sledge strong and true,
it's in my garage now forever to keep.

When I left school so much good advice,
guiding me to a worthwhile career.
Still I recall misbehaving,
and getting a clip round the ear.

Ah such happy times and memories,
alas these are not my own.
For I never knew who my father was,
as a young lad I had to face growing up alone.

No kind word or reprimand,
or father and son celebrations when I turned eighteen.
To all who have and know their dad,
you are fortunate, for I will never know what should
have been.

Dave Wilkie

DAD - FOUR MONTHS ON

There's spring in the air, Dad; the daffs are all through.
I dug the garden today, and weeded it too.
Lyn planted broad beans, as she always used to,
When she planted them for you, Dad; she planted them for you.

We're gardening early, and it's not looking bad;
But looking around here makes me quite sad.
For the strawberries, the raspberries, the plums (good and bad!) -
We picked them for Dad, Lyn; we picked them for Dad.

The kids had a fun day, as they always do.
The garden, a Sunday, their friends - heady brew!
They're happy enough, but it's certainly true
That they really miss you, Dad; they really miss you.

Some souls must look down with the wise and the just,
And some must look up from the ashes and dust.
But you'll always look straight - as a gentleman must -
And you lived life for us, Dad; you lived life for us.

Ian Hodgkinson

SO NEAR, YET SO FAR

Through all my life you have stood by me
And cared for what I thought
Through thick and thin you have tried to give
The answers that I've sought

Whenever I have needed help
A shoulder on which to cry
You have always been a tower of strength
And helped me to get by

I sometimes wish we didn't live
This great distance apart
I hope you know although not near
You are always in my heart

I miss you Dad and even though
You are just a call away
I wish I could awake each morn
And see you every day

I love you lots and though at times
I know I've made you sad
We have also had the best of laughs
I'm glad that you're my dad

Stephanie L Griffiths

MY DAD

I don't care what doctors say
My dad's not a poorly man
My dad will live forever
Just because I know he can
My dad you see is special
Just because he is my dad
So I've no need to worry
No reason to be sad
I don't care what doctors say
I know my dad will never leave
My dad will live forever
Because that's what I believe
My dad you see is special
So all he needs to know
To make him always be there
Is that I love him so.

Sue Hind

DAD

Left with only memories
Most of them are good
I hope I have behaved the way
A dutiful daughter should

For life for me goes on now
Memories are all I have to show
To remember a wonderful dad
Who I have had to let go.

You are no longer here with us
At last we had to say goodbye
Links of a loving family are never broken
I know in eternity we'll meet again
We'll be reunited you and I.

Elizabeth Amery

GOODBYE DEAR FATHER

Goodbye dear father. No! No, not goodbye
For how could any love so strong be dead?
The wasted body hidden from my eye
Has loose'd its lively spirit but not fled.

I feel your presence reaching out to me
As drawn close to the coffin I must stand.
Turned inward is my grief in misery,
Oh how I long to touch it with my hand

As though by touch I could set back the clock
To feel your loving warmth just once again
Cancelling out this deeply crushing shock
And giving back the hopes that were in vain.

The universe is stilled and every molecule of air
Seems to have taken on a solid form,
To make a link between the body lying there
And my distracted love with sorrow torn.

The month of May did give you birth
When new life budded all around
But now in death February's cold earth
Awaits your ash on frozen ground.

How can I say my last goodbye
With flowers that will fade so soon.
The hymn that once moved me to cry
Is now an empty idle tune.

Nothing can reach me father dear
As deep inside myself I stay,
Only the presence of you near
Will help me through this bitter day.

Hilda M Norden

ODE TO A SEAFARING MAN

Broke the morn before the burning blaze
Drank the rising dank dew,
Then tilted the earth and fed his flock
Before having anything to chew.
>   That was my dad.

Mind as broad as the flicker of light
Patience as calm as the dead sea,
His natural smile was a wonderful sight
His conscience like a bird, was free.
>   That was my dad.

Daily set ablaze his twisted plug!
Watching the rings drift and grow,
Waving them from his blinding eyes
And settling it to a heart warming glow.
>   That was my dad.

Reeled off some west wind tales
Of how drifting ships dipped,
And ghosts clinging to the deck rails
Log shouldered and rabble lipped.
>   That was my dad.

Spoke about the violent billow foam
The white froth that made him sick,
Faced the world without owing any man
And never twisted a juggler's trick.
>   That was my dad.

Francis Hughes

LIFE OF YESTERDAY

The man I once knew was fit and strong,
Arms stretched to catch me if I went wrong,
His hands were big, his shoulders broad,
He bought me all sorts he couldn't afford;
Head held high, eyes sparkling bright,
Tucked me in before saying goodnight.

Now the old man sits a drawn look upon his face,
Trying to forget the human race,
Shoulders quite bent, hair thin and grey,
Remembering life of yesterday.

The man I once knew stood ten feet tall,
My Prince Charming, no one else mattered at all,
He made me feel happy when I felt sad,
He'd even scold me if I were bad,
He would be unhappy when I cried,
Then wipe away the tears from my eyes.

Now the old man sits a drawn look upon his face,
Trying to forget the human race,
Shoulders quite bent hair thin and grey,
Remembering life of yesterday.

He lifts his head and smiles at me,
It's the same old smile it's always been,
He may be old and tired of life,
He's seen many times of trouble and strife,
But there's been lots of happy times too,
Memories for me and for you.

Sitting remembering,
The life we once had,
He's still my Prince Charming,
My dear old Dad.

Jenny Martin

MY FATHER

When I was a child he played all of my games,
Once older, his opinions, reflected my aims,
Only he could make me truly smile or cry,
Clearly see reason, not having to try,
I could rely on no man as I could on him,
Listened with earnest to my troubles, my every whim,
No man could match his humour, or ever stand as tall,
Advised always readily, from experience, gave his all,
No man could gain my respect as he,
Sat in deep silence, when I needed to be,
I held that man in high esteem,
That man, the maker of my dream,
Now, taken from me, I am as though without a limb,
My mind not as sharp, my thoughts they dwell on him.

Helen Sanders

DEAR DAD

Dad is a person, we all take for granted
His busy work schedule often keeps us apart
Coming home weary, exhausted and tired
On his favourite chair, Dad fell asleep by the fire

Trying hard to earn an honest living
There for us, someone who was always giving
His sound advice for every day life
Preparing us for decisions in our own adult life

I remember Dad in those earlier days
From childhood piggy-backs to my own wedding day
When Dad grew old, frail and ill
Sad to see his health decline, I loved him still
We cried, we grieved, he passed away
Thanks for everything *Dad*, what more can I say.

Rita Humphrey

THANKS DAD

I remember your stern and grumpy face
I remember your angry shout
I remember refusals of money
When I wanted to go out
Perhaps you saw what I couldn't then
When you kept me in at night
Away from harm and danger
I know now you were right
I remember too a face that smiled
At 'Daddy's little treasure'
All the love you gave me
No one could ever measure
You brought me up your own sweet way
You've done your best for me
I'm proud to call you daddy
You mean the world to me.

Andrina Couper

DAD

Walked down memory lane today,
Stood there speechless, not knowing what to say.
Last time we were here with our Dad,
No longer with us, makes us sad.
But, we know Dad now lives with you,
Sits at your feet, prays, worships too.
One day we'll all be together again,
And we too with you will reign,
See our Dad, face to face,
Yet another gift of grace.

Carol Pattinson

CHILDHOOD MEMORIES

Memories of our Dad
          are a thing of the past,
We try and hold on to
          for as long as they last.

I'd always think of him
          icing the cakes
And busy baking
          for all to take.

The turkey dinners and
          Sunday roast,
There the things, I liked
          the most.

He'd always sit with
          a cheeky grin,
The sweat pouring
          to his chin
The oven in the kitchen
          was his best mate,
There was nothing in it
          he couldn't create.

Of my Dad, the memories,
          will never fade,
He'll always be standing
          in my shade.

Sylvia Roberts

TO DAD WITH LOVE

You have always been such a great support to us,
Waved Mother's excesses aside when she made such a fuss;
We could twist you around our little fingers, or so we had thought,
To get what we wanted when Mother refused us, and how we fought.

Nesting on your back as you rode through the countryside,
With you life seemed great, when Mother called out to us we'd hide;
These bicycle hikes, picnics and foreign trips galore,
Life with you as a child was great, who could have asked for more!

As we grew older you became so much sterner,
The good life, it seemed, was placed on the back burner;
You gradually succumbed to Mother's mode of discipline,
And I bonded more closely with Jane my only sibling.

Birthdays and Christmases were sheer delight!
When you appeared as Santa Claus you were a wonderful sight!
The children at school never guessed who you were -
In those days of new equality, neither him nor her.

We were always proud to be seen out with you,
You never looked drab, your clothes always seemed brand new;
Your manners distinguished you as one of the Kings of Men -
Invitations to you almost always ended in, 'Do come again.'

On my wedding day you beamed with such pride,
As I walked down the aisle with you the silver tiaraed bride;
David was so proud to call you his father-in-law,
You, with reservations, had remarked, 'What on earth in him you saw?'

Your grandchildren gather around you and old memories come rushing back,
The goodness of life you'll instil in them, nothing they will lack;
I'm so happy and proud that you are proud of me, your daughter -
And I am prouder still to have you as My Father.

Margaret Andrews

DAD AT WORK

Dad did manual work for a living
Farm worker, iron moulder, collier was he
His best effort was bent on giving
To support his wife and family

He had to rise early in the morning
He would behold the bright rising sun
Another long day of work was dawning
He would be aching when it was done

Dad would sweat and toil for ages
Quenching his thirst with sweet cold tea
His lunch was wrapped in newspaper pages
This was the way he provided for me

The bus is waiting the engine beating
Ready to take workers home for their rest
The fire is blazing the family is eating
This is the time Dad liked best

Two young lads and three little girls
Sit at the table and they look up at Dad
He reaches down and ruffles their curls
And talks of the kind of day he's had

E M Sheppard

MY DAD

Whatever problems I have known
And there've been quite a few
My Dad was always there for me
And helped me see them through.

When people didn't understand
The troubles that I had
He'd always take me by the hand
I love him lots, my Dad.

His words are always comforting
His wisdom knows no bound
The surest way of finding out
Is ask my Dad, I've found.

So raise your glass and drink a toast
To the octogenarian lad
The finest man in all the world
I'm proud to call him Dad.

Jane Hewitt

WILLIAM JOHN THOMAS

Strong and fair, a rock to build our future on
someone to look up to and be proud, that was you
Dad a quiet giant, never brash never loud.
In childhood you were our teacher, our protector
and always our best mate.
Then when our world collapsed, and you became both
Dad and Mum, 'No one was to blame' you said,
it was just cruel fate.
The adolescent years that followed, we didn't always
agree, you were still my best mate, the only pain
was me.
But still we muddled through, my marriage was the
turning point, and my first break with you.
Then my own family came along and once more you
were there, as Grandad's went you proved to be the
one that was rare.
A King among men loved and adored, with your kind
brown eyes and silver hair.
Now all that's left is an empty chair, a thousand
memories and a million tears,
A family that loved you, and a daughter that wishes
you were still here.

Carol Irving

FRANK

When I was only 18 months old, my Mother was denied of her life,
Leaving my brother and me, and taking from our Dad, his wife.
We were then classed as orphans and went to live with our Grandma,
Though Dad tried to change her, he didn't get very far.

Though he worked every day, of money there was never enough,
Looking after us was a task, he must have found it very tough,
He had a curvature of the spine, and one leg was shorter than the other,
But there as nearly always a smile on his face, unless we gave him any
                                                              bother.

Quite soon things got too much, he had to admit he couldn't cope,
I was put into Banardos, taking my toothbrush, flannel and soap,
Over the years I saw my Dad often, my brother used to visit as well,
I noticed pain in my Dad's face, he was ill, I could tell.

I got married when I was 18 years old, my Dad was proud and gave me
                                                              away,
I'll never forget the joy on his face, I still remember it to this day,
Quite unexpectedly I had a phone call, from my brother, breaking the news,
Dad had been rushed into hospital, but typical Dad, I knew the nurses
                                                    he would amuse.

After a couple of weeks he was discharged, sent home to recuperate,
Doctors told us there was no hope, his health would soon deteriorate,
A week later he died, due to heart failure, the result of his curving spine,
It made it difficult for him to breathe, at age 53, his heart gave up for all
                                                              time.

Glennis Horne

FATHER'S DAY

Father's Day is a day to cherish,
A day when children learn to give,
However small it's the thought that counts,
I wish there were more like the day above.

For days before the children save
Which shop can I go to
And what can I buy?
Oh, Daddy loves chocolate and so
do I!

Joanna Littlejohns

MY FATHER

I love my father
and he said he loved me, once
but he left me
when I was an infant.

I've missed him most
on Mother's Day
when other children were buying presents
with their fathers
and I had to do it alone.

Now I am older
I try to understand
can you love somebody
and not ask for years
how are they doing?

I never thought of him badly
though he never played with me
or saw me for years
except he cried
every time he met me.

I am a part of him
but he has never been
a part of my life
so I think I love him as I ought to
and not because I know him.

Silvia Kufner

DAD AND THE TELEVISION SET

My father adores his TV set.
They make a lovely pair!
If the house burnt down about him,
He wouldn't know or care.

Disturb him at your peril!
Please don't even try!
He's lost in contemplation
Of that ever changing eye.

With the remote control beside him
And the TV guide to peruse,
He watches anything that's on,
But he cannot miss the news.

Every hour on the hour,
His body-clock is set.
He does it automatically.
He hasn't missed one yet!

He's appalled by the murders
And shocked by every sin.
It confirms his view of the world
And the terrible state it's in.

What can be done with him?
He's really hooked!
How can we cure him?
What have we overlooked?

Well, he doesn't drink or smoke,
And he's really rather nice.
So I think we must allow him
A solitary vice.

Nicola Barnes

DAD

Oh Dad if you could only see the things that I have done
I know you'd be very proud of me as you're oldest son
But you died when I was nine years old
I just cried my heart out with no-one's hand to hold

Winning the County Cup and scoring all four goals
Nobody on the touchline on your side to cheer, makes scoring a heavy load
Had you been there cheering me on from the side
Perhaps that would have made me happy instead of my feelings jumbled
up inside

When I ran a four-minute mile at sixteen it should have been a great day
in my life
But it really didn't mean a single thing, just another day into a dark night
No encouragement - no-one behind me to give me a little shove
I've often wondered to myself if you were watching from above

Events in life - Eighteenth birthday - 21st birthday - passing my driving test
These were just day to day events when they should have been the best
Guidance you could have given to put me on to the right road
Life was very tough for me - and anything worthwhile I had to hold

When you died, I grew up fast, sort of overnight
I had no one to turn to, no-one to sort my battles out, so I would have to fight
It really made me bitter when I see what other kids had got
They had everything and all the things that I had not

In moments of peace and quiet I often think of you Dad
And how I was robbed so young of the love and affection I should have had
Would things have been a lot different, had you lived a little longer
Would I be a different person - maybe wiser maybe stronger.

Leigh Smart

MY FATHER

It wasn't until my father had died
That I appreciated him and I cried
I remembered so well his homely wit
And the wisdom that always accompanied it
Now years later I often recall and say
Many of the things that he said day after day
'There is nobody in the world that's better than you
And remember you are no better, remember that too.
The grass is not greener the other side of the hill
Scratch on your own midden and you'll come to no ill
When you're not hungry and when you're not cold
These are the things that are better than gold
If you can't praise someone without any gall
Then better say nothing, nothing at all.'
Many were the homespun words that came from his mind
God fearing, hard working and most generously kind
It's taken me many years to realise his worth
This lovely good man who gave me my birth
If only I had him back and could say
'Yes, father, yours was the better and only true way.'

Edna May Whiter

PLAY IT AGAIN

'Daddy's home' was his familiar call,
As he stumbled and fell against the wall.
Beer filled breath would fill the room,
As he'd head for the piano to play a tune.

Two little girls, one was me,
Jumped out of bed for daddy to see.
Scrambled downstairs, eager to please -
'Come and dance to my music' daddy would tease.

There stood the piano, we sat on top,
Mum getting frantic 'Tommy please stop'
Daddy would sing all his favourite songs,
We'd got to know them, so we sang along.

You weren't always good, I know that now,
But our musical nights were special somehow.
So wherever you are, I'd just like to say,
Your old favourite songs -
Are my favourite today.

Vanessa A Hulme

UNTITLED

I never really told you Dad, of all the many times
I leaned upon your wisdom, and your honour in my prime,
I knew thro' good times, and the bad your hand would steer me well.
Even when you asked 'What's wrong my dear I wouldn't really tell.'

The growing years were precious times I thought they'd never end,
I tried to change some golden rules, but found they would not bend,
I asked you why these rules were made, and held in such revere,
You gently took me by the hand, and said 'I love you dear.'

The grown up years came all too soon, and you seemed wiser Dad,
The standards now my way of life, weren't really all that bad,
My trust in you, and yours in mine, became a lovely thing,
I knew I couldn't hurt you Dad, or any sorrow bring.

Altho' today you are at rest, I hope you feel some pride,
That I have never let you down, or cast your rules aside,
I should have told you how I cared, and spoken of my love,
But looking upwards to the sky - your smile comes from above.

Doreen Cruickshanks

TO DAD

We had a lot of fun together
You, my Dad and I.
Recently when you were very old
From when I was knee high.

You were a patient listener.
Your advice was always good.
We went for many lovely walks
As often as we could.

For years we went to football
To support Ipswich Town.
And even when they lost the game
It never got us down.

As you grew old and your health failed
You were like my little boy.
I had to run your life for you
But to help you was a joy.

And now you've gone to heaven
So I miss you every day.
But I know one day we'll meet again,
Then you'll never go away.

Elizabeth Smith

POEM FOR DAD

When I was young I remember, going
For a Sunday walk,
With my Dad, through woods we'd stalk.

Trees tall, grass so green,
Come across a shallow stream,
Dad would look down at me and with a beam
Take my hand and say, 'Ain't life just grand.'

As I got older my dad taught me to be
Much bolder. He gave me strength and
Courage, and his shoulder.

My Dad and me thought it would be
For eternity, unfortunately for my Dad
It was not to be,
So to the garden of rest,
For my Dad,
He was the best.

Carol Anne Risdale

FATHER'S DAY '89
NEWCASTLE MEADOW. MY DAD'S DREAM, IN HIS MEMORY

I have a dream, which will unfold.
A special story never told.
A winding road.
A country lane.
A field within the very same.

Here is a very courageous man.
Who built a dream upon his land.
He fed the dogs,
And took the view.
He loved to be there all year through.

He'd wander down that country lane
To a little pub with a similar name.
A friendly face would greet him there.
Everyone is so sincere.

He stops awhile and then returns.
To the piece of land for which he yearns.
Newcastle meadow is its name.
Our special feelings will always remain.

Kay Johnson

SPECIAL MEMORIES

Blue eyes sparkling, that childlike, boyish grin,
playing cards and dominoes, trying hard to win.
'Knobbly Knee' contests, white legs with rolled down socks,
telling us to be quiet, horse-racing on the box.
Working hard, two jobs, five hungry mouths to feed,
never getting time to rest, or consider your own needs.
Summer day trips to Skegness, Sundays at Bradgate Park,
firework displays at the Abbey Park Show, bonfires in the dark.
Hearing the sound of your Honda, hearing your key in the door,
a leather smell on your work-clothes, rich memories of the poor.
Party games and silly tricks, your story of Twycross Zoo,
of how you teased the 'Lion Tamer' but the last laugh was on you.
Christmas Days were special, Birthdays were never forgot,
even though there wasn't much money, you gave us such a lot.

I'd love to hear your Honda now, come speeding down the street,
I know that day will have to wait, until in Heaven we meet.
All these little memories are special because of you,
I had a special childhood and you were special too.

Wendy Nethercot

THE DIGGER
(For Douglas Rae)

You picked him out gently,
Felt the power in him
Brushed the dirt away.
The trap held no blood
He was firmly anchored,
Still the paws were set
To churn up the earth.
It was all about tactics
Knowing the complex labyrinth
Must reach the river bank.

The rain had been heavy
Leaf mould and wet grass
Joined the fresh life
Wormed into the sparrow's song.

I remember when younger
Being hoisted up so high,
The same powerful shoulders
Which carried me for miles
Had helped build a sand castle.
This was supposed to be
A lesson in destruction.
You gently caressed him -
Locked between thumb and forefinger
The movement was barely perceptible.

Maureen Macnaughtan

A POEM TO MY DAD

My dad he seems to always scold,
But really has a heart of gold.
He likes to make things out of wood,
And at this job he is very good.
If you want a good cook don't pick my dad,
And with this choice you'll be very glad!
My dad seems to know even more than me,
I guess he must be smart you see.
He also likes all kinds of sports,
And going to visit old ancient forts.
My dad likes to think he's fit,
But he'll probably get there bit by bit.
So dad I'd just like you to know,
That we'll still love you wherever we go.

Louise Turner (13)

GONE BUT NOT FORGOTTEN (MY DAD)

My Dad was a Canadian guy, 6ft wide and 6'2" tall
Came over here in the forces joined up of his own accord
Took an active part in the Second World War,
When the Germans came 'knocking' on our front door.
He met my Ma along the way, asked her to marry him nearly straight away.
Eventually married, my oldest brother born, Dad went back to Canada for his demob.
Mam joined him later in this strange land, me and my younger brother eventually 'came along'
Five years later over to England we came, Ma was homesick, and Dad the same
My Dad a qualified mechanical engineer but! His qualifications weren't recognised over here.
But my Dad was a grafter wouldn't let owt beat him
At in International Harvester he soon got a job, where everyone came to rely on him
A real Jack of all trades mending tellies cars and bikes,
watches, also woodwork anything you like
Working 15 hours a day an occasional day off, and so,
They'd hire a local bus, neighbours too, then off to the seaside we would go.
My Dad taught me woodwork and how to mend bikes, a very patient man quiet too, whom everybody liked
If he couldn't buy a part from the scrapyard, he made it himself didn't find it hard
The English climate and arthritis became his downfall, had to finish his job, sometimes he could only crow (literally)
My Mam a good cook, my Dad even better, he taught me to sew and was a real good knitter.
When he died there was no legacy, but! All these trades he passed down to me
Neighbours still remember my Dad and all the things he'd do
When I go past the local timber yard, oh the smell of wood, I remember him too.

Sandra Witt

A TRIBUTE TO MY FATHER

High on the Rock my father lies,
Long buried 'neath the Spanish sun,
Nearby Gibraltar apes catch flies
And sailors seek the night-club fun.

Two hours before I first saw light
My father's injuries took toll,
Others too suffered the same plight,
Their names to join the Navy's scroll.

'An accident aboard the ship'
The Admiralty Board reported,
Later I saw his pension slip,
Medals and photos kept assorted.

When I was young I often thought
Would he have played with me at ball,
Or trains or simple lessons taught
Or Hide and Seek when I was small?

He was but thirty when he died,
A Lieutenant Engineer RN,
My mother often sat and cried,
A nanny came to tend me then.

Appointed to a teaching post
My mother might show me a token
Of their marriage, three years at most,
By word his name was never spoken.

A sailor then in World War Two,
Just as the sun began to dim,
My father, though I never knew,
I climbed the Rock to visit him.

Donald Burt

DAD

Once black, now grey,
More lucid now than it ever has been.
The toll of time and crosses heavy bared
Profoundly casual from bank to bank
You stride life's erratic stream.
Bewildered, contented belief.
Your faith built a home, imbedded in my heart
From which I can never, ever be torn apart.
Plastered you never were, and many a mould you made
Always and still there
In my mind blind kindness and awareness,
Between the lines a story of truth you always find.
Worldly wealth so far illusive
Your acceptance of greatness comes from worlds of different kind.
Pure, pure love with nature you bind,
A need for petrol leaves others far behind.
With dauntless courtesy to protect yours
You never shied and your option to offend
You always denied,
In sickness and in health
You have constantly helped me to find myself.
No leash, just trust of the like
In my life's journey, I have never met.
In the pain, strain, and mind numbing bombardment of life
Your path illuminated, sober you stand straight
Unpretentious, radiant with authentic grace.
You are my strength, my light, my hope
And ever present the words,
Love, honesty, family, honour, kindness, strength
And hero -
Immortal you do provoke
Dad.

Kenneth Leddy

DAD

Once my father sat me on his knee
And rocked and soothed till my tears were free.
A child grown, troubled beyond belief,
Dad was my source of blesséd relief.
He shared my pain, suffered in my stead
The nightmare thoughts raging round my head.
The hurt I knew melted for a while,
Releasing my sadness so I could smile
My father always, to the very end!
My very best and dearest friend!

Wendy P Frost

THANK YOU DAD

Thank you for showing us the wonders of nature around us
For teaching us the names of each bird and flower
For making us appreciate the good things in life
And not to be consumed by money and power

Thank you for showing us right from wrong
For teaching us that compassion and forgiveness go hand in glove
And for always making us feel so special
For your kindness, patience and especially your love

I know we don't say thank you nearly enough
Or tell you how much we care
But I'm sure you know how much we love you
And appreciate you always being there

On your 'Special Day' we send your way
Our grateful thanks for all you do
We wish you years of health and happiness
For we are so proud to have a dad like you

Patricia Waters

UNTITLED

My Dad is so special,
there's no one who comes near
I must admit when I was young,
he was one I would fear.
His five little daughters,
All pristine and looking fine,
Mum would make us identical clothes,
and stand us neat in line.
Half our life spent playing,
on the boundary watching cricket.
Just in case, by a stroke of luck,
Dad would take a wicket.
The ball was showered round the ground
fours and sixes everywhere.
They would shout oh no it's Jack again,
and stare into the air!
We're all grown up now and daughters I have two,
though husband I have no longer.
through thick and thin my dad's been there,
to make me feel somewhat stronger.
It's taken some years to get on my feet,
without dad I couldn't have done it,
through sad days, bad days, often many
I'm still here just to prove it.
There aren't enough words to express,
the affection that I have,
So I'll tell you in my poem,
I love you, thanks for being my dad!

Jacqueline M Williams

DAD

I know that I have you to thank
For what I am today.
You've shown me by example
What to do and what to say.
I admire your many talents,
You're honest and sincere,
You always do your best for us,
On each day of the year,
No one could be more needed,
Thanks is what I want to say,
For the many things you've done for me,
Which I never can repay.

Kathleen Elliott

FATHER'S DAY

My father he is special, and loves me very much
Even when I'm naughty and he has to say 'Don't touch'.

He gives my mother money to buy the food we eat,
And if there's some left over, then I might get a treat.

When the sun is shining, we both go for a walk
And if we find a little seat, sometimes we sit and talk.

I hope he likes the present I've bought for 'Father's Day',
But even if he doesn't, he'll thank me anyway.

I think I will surprise him on this his special day.
I'll help him in the garden and put my toys away.

My father, he is special, so on this Father's Day
I'll send this message to him, 'Thank you' is what I say.

Angela Constable

MY DAD TED

With nervous heart and shaking limbs
Tears falling from his face,
My father watched my birth in awe
A birth of easy grace.
His builders hands so rough and coarse
Held mine so thin and small,
His ears alert to every sound
A cry my favourite call.
When small he taught me how to walk
And caught me when I fell,
The chemist shop he'd visit if
I ever felt unwell.
In teenage years he was my friend
And 'Dad'! I need a lift',
He'd lecture me on boys and friends,
A special father's gift.
He'd worry if I came home late
My virtue he'd defend,
Until one day my dad's heart broke
I'd found a special friend.
The man I'd met would be my love
But never take his place,
A son he'd gained to share his life
Pride shining on his face.
I love you dad and always will
True flesh and blood that's we,
You've proved your love a million times
So selflessly to me.

J Byrne

FATHER'S DAY

Happy Fathers Day and love to you,
I wish you joy in all you do.
You deserve a really lovely day
Cause you're so kind in every way.
You're just so very good to me,
You're like a dad should always be
You've really got a heart of gold
It's not often enough, you are told
You mean so much to me you know
And so much love you always show.
I love you each and every day,
I love you in every possible way
I love you so much I'd like to say
Have a really lovely Fathers Day.

Helen Mousley

DADDY AND ME

I love my daddy in a special way
I love the times when we laugh and play
I love to see him smile every day
But then the fun stops as we drive away
I know that my daddy loves me too
And when we go home he
Thinks that his life is through
He wants every day to be his last
To make up for the pain
He has caused us in the past
But if he goes we would all
Miss him oh so very badly
And no longer can us kids
Say to him 'We love you Daddy.'

Alan Brindle

DAD

The love that binds my heart to you
Is like an everlasting glue
You're so precious in my heart
It pains me when we are apart
You're so special, always there
Helping me, you always care
The best mate that I ever had
You never shout, you're hardly mad
It brightens up my every day
Whenever Daddy walks my way.

Sharon Reilly

IF I COULD BE LIKE YOU

When folk look at me
My father they say is what they see
If only that could be half true
I'll never be as good as you.

Remember the rose you chose for me
The cuddle and kiss for my skinned-up knee
Afraid of the dark and the grizzly bear
I'd awaken in fear, you were always there.

Clever and smart, wise and good
If I could be like you, I wish I could
You taught me so much, put me on the right road
Drummed into me, an ethical code.

To me you're a king, an honourable man too
I even thought God took advice from you.
Is there anything you can't do?
Oh my dad, I'm so proud of you.

T Bellamy

I WANT . . . TO SAY THANKS DAD!

Here I begin my usual phone call,
'Ring, ring', Hi dad, how's you, mum and all,
'Hi, Kim again, okay what do you want?'
'Don't worry dear dad, not near to a lot'.
Just . . . teabags, cheese, bread and meat,
Perhaps something from your freezer to eat,
Toilet roll, washing powder, milk for tea,
I'm sure one day you will give me a fee.
Compost, peat and the plants with it.
Not to forget plant pots, only want a bit.
Demi-johns, sugar and mix for the wine,
Help to cook my barbecue, you'll be fine,
Oh I need some butter and some eggs,
Plain flour, caster sugar and nutmeg,
Spirit level, tape measure and your help
to drill holes to put up our shelf.
Just a lift in your car to here and there,
How about lending your garden chairs.
Wallpaper paste . . . your pasting table
and decorate please cos we're not able.
The list could go on, never end,
I don't want to ask 'Give us a pen!'
And every Saturday you buy me a paper,
I don't really think fee's will come later,
All what you do dad is because you care,
And to the world I want that to share,
You are loved, in our hearts so very much,
If I call, I may 'want', but also want to keep in touch,
By the way, I would like, I mean I want . . .
To say thanks Dad! I mean that lots!

K A Ashcroft

MY DAD

My dad
A man I've always had
I hope he'll always be there
for me to love and to care

We sing together
      laugh together
hopefully for ever and ever!

When we're apart
he fills up my heart

When we're near
it seems so clear
that he's my dad.
The *best* man I've ever had.

Krista Brocklehurst

MEMORIES

Although we bickered, argued and fought,
I loved you Dad, more than you probably thought.
Sometimes we seemed too alike to get on,
And neither of us wanted to say that we were wrong,
But Dad you were gentle and loving and kind,
And these memories I mustn't let slip from my mind,
For you were a brave and wonderful man,
And said I must do the best that I can,
You cared for me, and wanted me to succeed,
And to have you with me is the thing that I plead,
It doesn't seem fair, you were taken away,
For together our family was happy and gay.
But I try to remember, that although you have died,
You're gone from our sight, but not from our minds.

Emma Bignall (14)

SOME THOUGHTS OF DAD

Father did not show affection
In the cuddly sort of way
His love he surely showed us though
In many other ways
The early years were cycle rides
Beginning on his cross-bar saddle
Telling us this, showing us that
He loved his allotment garden
Vegetables for us all year round
Garden roses were his other loves
Later proud bunches for me
June through October
In my own home for all to see
Always busy with paintbrush or spade
For him not enough hours in the day
Holidays were another thing
South coast we always went
How did we ever manage
Just from two bulging suitcases - by train?
A soldier he never was - but
At home *up front* to volunteer
Memories last forever
But Dad's no longer here.

Maureen Brewer

MY DAD JACK

M y dad Jack was the best -
Y ou see I was truly blessed
  - with a
D ad in a million!
  - He was
A lways there to show he cared
  - that was my
D ad!

J ack Barnes was my dad
A nd a better one, no-one could have had.
C ruelly cancer took him before his time
K indness, caring - he was mine!

Elaine Duggan

TO DAD

The stories you told, at the end of my day
the kiss on the forehead, kept the goblins at bay.
The walks in the park, the rides at the fair,
my first day at school, you being there.

The telling off, for coming home late,
the fatherly talk, on my first date.
Drying my tears, when my heart was broken,
understanding, yet, no words spoken.

Worrying about the way I dressed,
making me laugh, when I was depressed.
Showing me the right path to take
helping me learn, by my mistakes.

Holding my arm, as we walked down the aisle,
seeing you proud, seeing you smile.
I want you to know that as long as I live,
I'm grateful, for the love, you had to give.

Linda Laband

MY FATHER

When I was very young,
I believed I had a guardian angel,
and I did not realise,
that the strong shadow,
which always protected me,
was my father's love,
watching over me.
And as my years increased,
I know I caused you to worry,
but I thought I could stand alone,
it took me a while to realise,
that the shadow was there again,
was my father's love,
watching over me once again.
Now I live quite far away,
I still know that deep down,
my father is always with me, -
his love is so unbounded,
and comes through thick and thin,
and I know that in his eyes,
I could never commit any sin.
His hands are so artistic,
and have produced many,
great and wonderful things,
because they helped to guide me,
in everything that I do.

Angela Craig

OUR DAD

He's worked all his life you know,
And now that he's retired,
He's often round at my house,
Whenever he's required.

He mows the lawns,
He mends things -
He baby-sits my child,
And now that I am on my own,
He stops him running wild.

He goes on about the old days,
When he was just a lad,
I'm on about the handyman,
The gardener,
My dad!

We cannot do without you,
And I want you to know,
You really are the best dad,
And we love you so.

Glynis Carr

DAD

Gone but not forgotten, you're with me all the time.
You're watching over everything I do.
I hear your happy laughter, I see your loving smile.
I feel your presence all around me too.

Gone but not forgotten, by everyone you knew.
The world around will be a sadder place.
Everybody loved you. 'A gentleman!' They said.
And everyone will miss your smiling face.

Gone but not forgotten, you're always on my mind.
I think of all the happy times you made.
I always will remember, your kindness and your love.
My memories of you will never fade.

Gone but not forgotten, you're in the air I breathe.
I know you'll try to turn the grey skies blue.
This empty ache inside me, has chilled my very soul.
I know you'll send the sun to warm me too.

Gone but not forgotten, you're always in my heart.
You'll be with me, whatever lies in store.
I'll miss you and I'll love you, forever and a day.
Gone - but part of me for evermore.

J Frost

DAD

Early in the morning light, he donned his cap, before the night was over
To go earn his pay, his first of many a gruelling day.
Just a boy, only twelve years old, young and afraid but did as he was told.
Of children, the oldest, his turn to go, and the very first morning
he hated it so.

The tunnels were black, no sunlight could show.
Explosions and dust, men kneeling down low, some trying to eat
With mice at their feet.
Ponies and carts trundled past, moving steady, shovelling was hard and
his arms grew heavy.
A light in the distance meant someone was there, but by the end of the shift,
He did not dare to think of next day and earning his pay.

Forty years on, the boy's now a man, no longer afraid he does what he can
To help those trapped, down deep in the dirt, not hearing the sirens,
just knowing they hurt.
Respected by all, not for his girth, for quiet strength and patience, he's
the salt of the earth.

If I was a writer, with talents untold, I'd tell more of his life, as
precious as gold.
'Cos I knew him and loved him all of my days, I wish I had more of his ways.
He made me happy, never sad.
He taught me good things, never bad.
We shared our thoughts without a word, just a look and a smile,
and no-one else heard.

Even when he grew grey and his face was pale and when the once-strong
legs began to fail,
Yet though he'd been up and in pain all night, when I asked how he was
he'd say 'I'm alright.'
With a gentle smile and a helping hand he'd always listen and understand.

I can still see him sitting there, before he passed away, and hear the words he
said to me that awful day.
'When I go please let me see, the birds and trees around.
I've spent enough years of my life deep down beneath the ground.'

He rests now, near the water side beneath the sky, where birds do glide
And flowers grow of every hue, some the colour of his eyes, so blue.
He's only gone from out of sight, his spirit's with me still.
He brought the sunshine to my life and I know he always will.

A gentle, kind and loving man with inner strength, and no-one can
Replace the love for me he had,
The boy, the man, my friend, my *Dad!*

Annette Walker

DADDY'S GIRL

I recall those happy days, when I was *Daddy's girl;*
When he would bounce me on his knee and set my heart a-whirl.
'Gee up Neddy' he'd sing to me as I listened to him there,
Up on my Daddy's knee, I never had a care.

Swiftly the time has rolled along and left me a treasure chest,
Filled with precious memories, the sweetest and the best.
When days are dark and dreary or I feel alone and sad,
I open up my treasure chest, given by a loving Dad.

I see my Daddy's smiling face, I see his dancing eyes,
Sparkling brighter than twinkly stars, more blue than summer skies.
I see his arms outstretched to me waiting to hold me tight,
Gently around me they'd securely fold,
Just like a blanket on a cold wintry night.

I hear his voice, the voice I love, I hear him call for me,
I'd claim a thousand welcomes when I'd run to Daddy's knee.
What fun we shared together, he was my special friend,
He gave enough love to last me until my journey's end.

Thank you for my treasure chest, for all, that has been mine,
Thank you for your kindness, your patience and your time.
Those happy days will never fade, my heart is still a whirl,
No need for words, I know it's true,
I'm still *my Daddy's girl!*

Eleanor Scott

DAD

A father is one of the few people,
We really get to know.
Through love and understanding,
Our affection for him will grow.

He's someone we can turn to.
With him there's no need to pretend,
He knows exactly what we're like,
And is a special friend.

The perfect understanding
Is a natural gift.
No matter what the problem is,
His support will never shift.

I learn by his experience,
Of missed opportunity and regret,
And so I have general guidelines,
And goals to be met.

Of course there are times
Of ill-feeling, a hatred of a kind
But this never lasts for long
And is easily put behind.

As I mature and grow older
So too does he.
But he will live for longer,
As he is part of me.

I unsurp the life from him.
Willingly he gives it to me.
And slowly he withers under the strain,
His sacrifice is not for free.

And when I know he means so much,
And for every moment I'm glad.
Why can't I say to him . . .
'I love you Dad!'

Máire Donnelly

A FATHER'S SOMEONE SPECIAL

Who's always there for you
He gives his love so freely
He is honest and he's true
His love will never falter
As the years go passing by
You can feel it in your heart
And see it in his eyes
He's a man you can always turn to
When troubles come your way
He would never turn away from you
His love is there to stay
So hold that love within your heart
And cherish it your whole life through
For it's a gift from heaven
That God has given you.

S J Watson

IN COMMEMORATION

My father was a Geordie, he worked hard, every day,
Taking any type of job - for a long day's pay;
Living through depression, the hunger marches rife,
The North-East and the dole queue, partnership for life.
My grandad did not want his son, so to a Seaman's Home
He went, lived life, day to day, without gripe or groan.

At fourteen years of age, they put him on a boat,
Off he sailed, to Canada, his heart was full of hope.
No home, no friends, an alien world that offered only despair,
He hoboed far across the land, worked for soup, not care;
A lumberjack in winter, sheep-shearer in the spring,
My father was a man with pride, he could do anything.

Returning to this country, when he was still a lad,
Heart, yet, full of hope - but, eyes so dull and sad.
Cutbacks throughout the land, a nation-wide depression,
He joined the ranks of the destitute, no recognised profession;
Once again, the hunger - defeating, bone-chilling cold,
Those days of pre-welfare state, 'Get a job,' he was told.

With pride, determined, once again my father found a job,
And, when the work ran out, he did not kill, nor rob;
With little memory of a home, even less of family life,
My father met my mother, found peace with his dear wife.
He is no longer with us, the tears I strive to fight,
Yet, comfort comes with a prayer - I talk to him, each night.

Good advice, he gave to me, and worldly, wise ideas,
That made me strong and honest - a woman with no fears.
I can never forget my father, nor, what his strength achieved,
He left behind, a daughter, proud and still bereaved,
Who loved him for his honesty - integral, loyal ways,
Still loves him with a constancy, for ever, and a day.

Pauline Allbright

HIS BEST BLOOMS

I stand and watch my father, unobserved from a door,
As he tends his beloved garden, enjoying every chore,
And my thoughts go back to a bygone day,
When he tended his children in a similar way.
With gentle hands he guided us,
Loved us when we fell from grace,
Encouraged us all to smile at life,
Whatever we had to face.
But most of all he gave himself,
So many of his hours,
He says they they were the best of times,
Spent with us . . . *his flowers.*

Eileen M Bailey

INFORMATION

We hope you have enjoyed reading this book - and that you will continue to enjoy it in the coming years.

If you like reading and writing poetry drop us a line, or give us a call, and we'll send you a free information pack.

Write to

Arrival Press Information
1-2 Wainman Road
Woodston
Peterborough
PE2 7BU